D0929806

MODERN FILING METHODS AND EQUIPMENT

G. CONTINOLO

MODERN FILING METHODS AND EQUIPMENT

Translated by Mary Bosticco
Edited by A. E. Phillips

BUSINESS BOOKS LIMITED
London

This work was first published in Milan, Italy, in 1966
under the title *Come organizzare l'archivo*
by Franco Angeli Editore

First published in the English language, 1970, by
Business Books Limited

© Guiseppe Continolo, 1966

© Business Books Limited, 1970

SBN 220 79937 7

*This book has been set in 'Monotype' Baskerville Series 169
and printed by C Tinling & Co. Ltd, London and Prescot
for the publishers, Business Books Limited (registered office:
180 Fleet Street, London EC4); publishing office: Mercury House,
Waterloo Road, London SE1*

Made and Printed in Great Britain

Contents

List of Figures

List of Plates

Introduction

I COLLECTION, SELECTION, CLASSIFICATION, PRESERVATION, SEARCHING

During the past 20 years the environment in which businesses operate has been changing rapidly. Companies have grown bigger, the work pattern has speeded up, markets have grown vaster, and business transactions in general have become more complex. As a result of all this, information has become considerably more mportant to the internal working of a business.

Nowadays an entrepeneur who really wants to consolidate his position in the market must act with as perfect a knowledge as possible of the factors influencing his decisions. In other words, nowadays success comes to those who operate in a rational manner and base each of their decisions on a solid factual platform.

In greater or lesser measure everyone has become aware of the need for this higher standard of performance and has consequently considered changing the organizational structure of his offices in order to meet this new need. However, those who carry out these changes do not always see clearly before them the objectives they wish to reach and the means they should use to attain them. The 'internal revolution' previously mentioned, has caught everyone by surprise. Ideas are lacking and in many cases even the necessary experience and this makes it difficult for many executives to realize this ambition, which they none the less sincerely believe in.

Let us therefore reiterate a few fundamental concepts.

In referring to the function of the modern office, we should make it clear first of all that nowadays it would be anachronistic to limit it to the collection and entry of the transactions and reports generated by the business. In effect the office is taking on more and more the aspect of a regular centre for the production of information. Therefore, while it must continue to collect the facts which are historically past, it must also integrate them with other facts obtained from other sources, elaborate them as necessary, making use of the most refined management techniques, and transform them into information which will be used to support the most important decisions which management will be called upon to make.

In this new business framework there are certain functions which, while they cannot be taken out of context, are especially important to the rationalization of the business and deserve to be examined separately. These functions are:

1 The collection of facts.
2 The selection from them of anything which may be useful to the business.
3 The orderly classification and preservation of the facts collected so that they will last for the length of time during which they will need to be consulted.
4 The retrieval of the facts collected and preserved for purposes of reference and elaboration.

2   THE IMPORTANCE OF FILING IN THE BUSINESS ORGANIZATION

The importance we have attached to these functions are due above all to the fact that the modern business is deluged by mountains of paper. Order forms, shipping bulletins, delivery notes, statistical and book-keeping forms, cheques, bills of exchange, statements, insurance policies, correspondence, internal memoranda—all are but examples of the various aspects which this phenomenon takes. Its immediate consequence is that administrative costs have risen sky high.

The processing of this enormous quantity of paper has become one of the main aspects of business activity. Or rather, everything which has to do with the processing of documents supporting the facts and figures of a business (*vide* the four functions listed above) deserve the particular attention of the people concerned with business management.

Having reached this conclusion, it becomes obvious that the object which merits our fullest attention is the filing cabinet, since that is where the documents containing the facts of interest to the business are collected, put in order, preserved, retrieved, and sorted. From the organizational point of view, therefore, the filing cabinet, which even in the past was of considerable importance, is now becoming one of the most sensitive areas of a business.

The term 'filing cabinet' obviously also includes filing techniques, which are losing their rule-of-thumb characteristics to take on a fundamental role in the interests of a more accurate process of information production.

Obviously a business filing system is not established for organizational purposes alone, but also for more traditional purposes, i.e. to satisfy the legal requirements. It is as well to make this point, since a substantial portion of the space in filing cabinets is occupied by documents and entries connected with the proper running of the business from the legal and fiscal points of view.

It may in fact be stated that the old and the new needs have jointly contributed to the importance of the filing system, an old concept which is still functionally up to date.

3 THE FUNCTIONS OF FILING

What are the functions of filing? In order to see the problem more clearly in its unquestionable relevance from the organizational point of view, it may be useful to recall these functions briefly to mind.

A filing system is usually set up in any kind of business to fulfil the following purposes:

1 To gather together in an orderly fashion all the documents which circulate in the business; particular stress should be put on the expression 'in an orderly fashion', since the proper functioning of the filing system depends precisely on the method adopted for putting the various documents in order.

2 To assure the perfect preservation of the documents collected; this function is carried out by the provision of the necessary equipment, i.e. cupboards, cabinets, shelves, temperature and humidity control apparatus, card-indexes, etc.

3 To retrieve documents quickly when requested by the various departments in the organization; in fact the success of the filing system depends upon the speed with which documents can be produced when needed by the various departments in the organization. Briefly, the filing system must become an active

information and documentation centre which serves the whole of the business.

4 To carry out the functions outlined above in the best and most economical way possible; a filing system can be considered well organized when it serves the organization well at the lowest possible cost.

Apart from these four main functions, there are secondary ones, such as making sure that the documents filed are in order, taking care of and sending out the mail (this frequently happens in small firms with small filing systems), taking care of the library and the reading room, and having forms, catalogues and booklets reprinted.

In order to carry out these aims it is obviously necessary to have an adequate organizational structure allowing for:

Sufficient competent staff.
Suitable premises to house the files.
Equipment suitable for the various needs.
The adoption of a rational filing system.
The organizing of the files according to fixed rules.
The appointment of a qualified person to take charge of the files.

4 THE PLAN OF OPERATION

The perfect organization of a filing system is not easy. In fact to set up a system which satisfies every need of the organization requires a great deal of knowledge that only a specialist can be expected to have.

The problem begins with the setting up of the files and the establishment of a system meeting both the legal requirements and the needs of the business. A choice must then be made on whether to adopt a centralized system or a decentralized one, active files or inactive files.

It will then be necessary to establish with great precision the criteria which will govern classification of the material, taking into consideration the various characteristics of the documents to be preserved and the various needs to which they will be put.

It will further be necessary to select the equipment best suited to the purpose and to work out the most suitable organization of the work to be carried out in the filing room.

Finally there is the problem of controlling all operations having to do with the filing.

The sum of the topics thus far alluded to represents the complex of knowledge needed in order to set up and put into operation a business filing system. These topics will be developed and dealt with in detail further on in this book, which also includes a section dealing with equipment which at some time in the future will permit radical changes in the setting up of a filing system, i.e. microfilm and electronic equipment.

The connecting link between each of these topics and the preceding one is the concern to fit the filing system into a rational organizational scheme which is not incompatible with the more general need to improve internal procedures within the organization. The need to transform business offices into an information-producing machine is too strongly felt to enable organizational problems to be seen as pertaining to independent departments without being harmful to the business as a whole.

Part I
NEED FOR A FILING AND CLASSIFICATION SYSTEM

1
THE FILING SYSTEM

1.1 STUDYING A SYSTEM

A file is a piece of equipment made to hold in an orderly fashion all documents whereon are entered all data and information of interest to the business, to preserve them perfectly, and to guarantee their prompt retrieval when needed by the various departments within the organization.

The most important part of this definition is that it makes clear, without the shadow of a doubt, that each company must adapt its files to its own particular purposes. This is deduced by the fact that the range of documents used in various businesses, even if they are in the same line, is extremely variable, as are the needs to consult them.

It follows that the choice of the most suitable system for a particular situation cannot be made in the abstract, but must be based on the exact business situation to which it refers. In other words, each company must first of all make a detailed study both of the documents to be filed and of the processes they will have to go through, before it goes on to seek out and set up a suitable filing system. Further, this preliminary investigation must not omit a study of the possible expansion of the company, since a filing system must continually adapt itself to the changing conditions in which the business operates.

Each company must therefore work out its own filing system, starting off by evaluating the following factors:

The types of material to be filed.
The reasons for filing it.
The quantity of material to be filed.
The staff available for filing work.
The equipment available.
Where the filing will be done.

When the filing will be done and how much time is available to do it in.

Future developments being considered for the filing work.

These factors must obviously be evaluated by bearing in mind two points: the degree of precision required in the classification and filing work and the cost involved in carrying out the plan.

1.2 THE TYPES OF MATERIAL TO BE FILED

The choice of a filing system must be influenced first of all by the types of material to be filed. It is obvious, for instance, that correspondence with customers has to be classified and filed in a different way from reports to top management, invoice copies, etc.

The first job to be undertaken, therefore, is the identification of the material to be filed, dividing it into homogeneous groups (with respect to content, source, object, length of time it will need preserving for, frequency of consultation, etc.). In any event the filing system must be as simple as possible and limited to few different groups. The more groups you have, the more complex will be the preliminary sorting job and the greater will be the opportunity for error.

Here is an example of the material normally contained in a file divided into groups:

Agents.
Banks.
Delivery notes (file copy).
Return notes (file copy).
Contracts.
Customer correspondence.
Supplier correspondence.
Customer invoices (copies for tax purposes).
Supplier invoices (originals for tax purposes).
Personnel.
Postal receipts.
Accounting documents.
Miscellaneous.

For each group of material an appropriate filing system will have to be established, bearing in mind the particular factors which distinguish each group, the principal factors being:

1 The value of the material: the higher the value of the material the more accurate must the filing system chosen be, to make sure it does not get lost and facilitate its retrieval;

2 Visual presentation of the material: every type of material has its own identifying features: number, date, name and address of customer or supplier in the case of invoices; name, address and date in the case of correspondence with customers, etc. The filing system chosen must require as little preliminary work as possible and must therefore bear in mind the characteristics of the material to be filed.

3 Number of times the material will probably be handled once it has been filed: if the material will not need to be handled again once it has been filed, a low-cost classification and filing system can be chosen; if, on the other hand, the material filed will constantly need to be consulted or otherwise handled, then a more exact system will have to be chosen, one which makes retrieval as easy as possible, even if this increases operating costs.

4 Length of time the material needs to be kept for: not all material needs to be kept for the same length of time and this time span will therefore influence the type of filing system to be chosen.

1.3 THE PURPOSES OF FILING

The specific purposes for which the material is filed determine which filing systems can be adopted. If, for instance, the object is to control the sales force, then there could be no better system than to file orders under the name of the salesman who secured them. If, on the other hand, the object is to indent the merchandise from stores, then the same orders could either be filed by delivery date or according to the merchandise ordered.

The purposes of filing must always be clearly defined, since when they are known it is always possible to select a system which fulfils the purpose in the best possible way and the lowest cost.

When, as is usual, the purposes are multiple, an optimum solution will have to be found, taking into consideration the various purposes in the best way.

1.4 THE QUANTITY OF MATERIAL TO BE FILED

The amount of material to be filed within a certain group can vary. When the amount is quite small, the filing system adopted can be simple in the extreme, without, however, losing sight of the other factors involved. When the opposite is true, then the filing system will have to be as detailed and precise as possible.

1.5 FILING STAFF

Responsibility for the filing can be entrusted either to specialized staff working full time or part time, or to non-specialized staff. In the first instance it is possible to select complex filing systems which require special training. In the second instance, the systems adopted must be as simple as possible, unified and conventional in order that the work may be carried out by staff without any particular training.

If, for instance, the filing is entrusted to specialized staff and a geographic classification is adopted, it will be possible to use a 'County–City–Borough' system, whereas, if non-specialized staff is used a classification into boroughs might result in considerable confusion.

1.6 EQUIPMENT AVAILABLE

If special equipment is available it is possible to select more complex and sophisticated filing systems. Otherwise it is advisable to choose one of the simpler systems, which enable the filing to be done more quickly and with a limited margin of error.

1.7 WHERE THE FILING IS DONE

If the filing is centralized, more elaborate filing systems can be used, since in this case it is more likely that suitable equipment and specialized staff are available and, in any case, the filing will be entrusted to a limited number of employees working under the supervision of a single person. If, however, the filing is decentralized, it is best to simplify the filing system as much as possible, in order to reduce the number of doubts, individual interpretations and other possibilities of error.

1.8 WHEN THE FILING IS DONE AND TIME AVAILABLE

Some filing jobs are carried out infrequently; others are done every day. For some, a great deal of time is allotted, others have to be completed as quickly as possible to enable other work to be done.

If the filing is done infrequently, the filing system has to be a simple one, since the people doing it cannot rely on a large backlog of experience. In the same way, if the time allotted to filing is limited, the filing system selected will need to be one requiring the least amount of handling and can be done more quickly.

1.9 PLANNING FOR FUTURE DEVELOPMENT

In working out a filing system it should be borne in mind that, once established, changes and modifications are to be avoided. Future developments in the company's needs, in general, and in the filing work, in particular, must therefore be borne in mind.

These developments cannot obviously always be foreseen with any degree of accuracy, and the more nebulous future needs are, the more flexible must the filing system be, so that it can adapt to the various possible contingencies with the minimum of change and upheaval.

1.10 THE ECONOMICS OF THE DIFFERENT SOLUTIONS

If there are alternative solutions, the most inexpensive one must be chosen. This apparently obvious criterion is, in fact, not easy to apply and is often neglected in favour of an abstractly more perfect or more 'advanced' one.

Filing is a service, that is, an activity which is not a means in itself, but is carried out to facilitate future work. It can therefore be said to be organized in an optimal way if it reaches its objectives in the best way, given the means and the working conditions at its disposal.

In order to achieve such a result it has to be borne in mind that filing requires staff, space, and equipment, all of which costs a great deal of money. It must also be borne in mind that the time required to retrieve and forward a document to the person requesting it often results in a loss of time for that person and that, in any event, waiting slows down work.

It is therefore advisable to:

Preserve only the indispensable documents.

Select a simple and quick filing system.

Companies often uselessly file between two and three times as many papers as they really need. This naturally causes bottlenecks, which are the main source of inefficiency in the office.

It follows that organizing the files in a business does not simply involve deciding on how to collect and put the documents in order, but mainly to establish rules for eliminating unnecessary ones.

In order to make sure that the filing system works smoothly all the time, it is necessary to provide for the elimination of all documents which have become useless and whose continued presence in the files only serves to encumber the whole filing service, without offering any compensating advantage.

The general rule which governs the economic feasibility of running a filing system establishes that *the total cost of filing a document (including retrieval costs) must be lower than the cost involved in doing without the document*. This axiom eliminates most of the doubts which could remain; it is obvious, to give but the simplest example, that a carbon copy of a letter accepting an appointment should be thrown away once the appointment has taken place.

In order to get satisfactory results in controlling filing costs, it is necessary to have considerable knowledge of filing techniques and of the filing equipment available. This knowledge must of course be used in harmony with the organizational structure of the business in which one is operating.

You should not, however, neglect to take into consideration the break-down of filing costs. According to fairly reliable estimates, it can be taken that 80% of total filing costs represent staff salaries, while the cost of filing equipment represents only 10% of the total. It is obvious, therefore, that considerable savings can be made simply by reorganizing the manual work involved along more rational lines.

In any event, savings in filing costs can be achieved by following the following instructions:

Check the reasons for which every form, report, letter, etc., has been created and eliminate useless originals and copies.

Prepare a filing system based on scientific classification and control techniques, which fully meets the needs of the business.

Provide for the installation of the most suitable equipment for the rapid filing of the documents.

Work out and adopt precise rules for the conservation, transfer, and consultation of the filed documents.

Delegate responsibility and authority for the filing.

It should not be forgotten, moreoever, that, as with most tasks, filing work increases in a geometric ratio to costs, as the degree of perfection required increases in arithmetical ratio. For instance, in order to have a classification by name in alphabetical order with 92–93% accuracy, it may be necessary to sustain a cost of, say, 100, which we can consider relatively low, since it will not involve laying down precise rules for carrying out the work or rigid controls on the work itself. In order to secure 95–96% accuracy, it will be necessary to establish exact classification rules and a simplified control system, which will increase costs up to at least 120–130.

In order to reach 98–99% accuracy, even more precise rules will be necessary, as well as better trained staff, more time, and more accurate control; costs would probably rise to 180–190. Even higher costs will be involved if next to absolute accuracy is demanded.

What applies to the degree of precision required also applies to the filing system adopted. Considerable increases in cost are involved in switching from one filing system to another, because of the greater number of operations involved, the greater complexity of the work involved, the more highly qualified staff required, etc.

Each system must therefore also be evaluated from the point of view of costs involved by asking the following questions:

Is is possible to obtain the same results by using other filing systems?

If we decide to simplify the filing system under consideration, will the disadvantages involved be compensated by the savings effected?

Are the costs of the filing work, as laid down by the system, compensated for by the advantages gained through the work?

Will a modification of the filing system enable simpler work procedures to be adopted with a consequent reduction in cost?

Does the filing system enable the work to be organized in an economical way?

1.11 SIMPLICITY AND SPEED

In the preceding paragaphs we have often stated that the filing systems selected must be as simple and rapid as possible.

We should like to point out, however, that all the filing techniques outlined in the chapter that follow are simple in theory and permit the filing to be done quickly. In practice, however, the attributes of simplicity and speed are conditioned by the following two factors:

1 The degree of familiarity with the filing system or systems which the filing staff has: the more familiar a system is and the longer it has been used, the more it will appear simple and quick. If there is not a degree of specialization in filing work within a company, it is unwise to adopt several different filing systems at the same time, since the technical advantages to be gained from it would be nullified by the lack of training in the filing staff involved.

2 The relative complexity of the filing system being considered: assuming a customer file, for instance, it is obviously simpler and quicker—unless considerable number of headings are involved—to file incoming correspondence alphabetically by customer name than to file it by county, city, borough, and then finally alphabetically by name.

The simplicity and speed of the filing systems adopted therefore depend to a considerable extent on how the classification systems adopted are used and co-ordinated.

1.12 CHARACTERISTICS OF THE FILING SYSTEM

To sum up it can be said that a filing system—bearing in mind the company's specific needs—must:

Facilitate as much as possible the work which follows classification.

Enable the filing to be done as simply and as quickly as possible with the minimum of staff training.

Stipulate the division criteria of the different categories or classes and the order of classification within each category, avoiding as much as possible doubts and subjective interpretations.

Indicate which are the categories or classes in which the material must be divided.

Bear in mind future needs and possess an adequate degree of flexibility.

1.13   THE FILING DEPARTMENT: A COMMANDING POSITION

In conclusion, it does not seem out of place to specify what the hierarchical position of the filing department should be in the organizational structure of a business.

If we bear in mind that another word for files is archives, from the Greek *arkhe*, meaning government, we shall readily see that we are confronted with an attribute of command. This implies that the conservation of documents must on no account be considered as a sub-species of warehousing and be abandoned, without control, to a store-keeper, as so often happens.

The selection of the official on whom the files must depend is a question of rank, which must be decided according to each individual case. The important thing is for the files to be put in charge of someone of sufficiently high level. This statement is valid for at least two reasons:

> In order that the problems connected with the files should not be considered as negligible *a priori*.

> Because only a central authority can have enough of an overview to make sure that the information contained in the files is used to the best possible advantage.

A connection with the general secretariat of the business, if such exists, would be most desirable from the point of view of the organization of the service. The essential, in any event, is that the filing department be suitably equipped and run and that its utilization be rationally organized.

A connection between the filing service and the O & M office (Organization and Methods) cannot fail to be advantageous. The O & M office is in a position of solving the problem of how to run the filing system economically, while a deeper knowledge of the filing problems will give the O & M office a better understanding of the facts which really interest the business.

2

CLASSIFICATION AND CODIFICATION

2.1 DEFINITION

To classify means to separate the material according to determined criteria with the object of:

Facilitating its retrieval.

Gaining greater knowledge of the material itself in order to enable a synthesis of its contents to be made—if necessary—or to analyse it more fully.

It can therefore be said that classification is a technique for the identification and systematic grouping of similar items, with common characteristics which can later be differentiated according to their fundamental types.

The identification and, secondly, the grouping of similar items with common characteristics are the main purposes of classification. This obviously presupposes the existence of distinctive characteristics enabling each item to be differentiated from the one before it.

Such characteristics can usually be gleaned directly from the documents to be classified. It frequently happens, however, that special symbols have to be devised in order to make the classification more satisfactory. In other words, it is necessary to think up a symbol to be affixed to each document to differentiate from the next one. This necessity arises when the difference between the documents is difficult to see or to interpret, but above all when special machines have been used (such as accounting machines or punched cards) which make it necessary to identify the operations in some way, thus obviating the limitations of such equipment.

According to current terminology, *codification* is the word used to indicate the act of applying the symbols and *code* is the system of symbols used. More precisely codification can be defined as the allotment of numbers, letters or other symbols, according to a systematic plan, in order to distinguish the category to which each item belongs and to distinguish one item from another, within the compass of the various categories.

2.2 IMPORTANCE OF A SYSTEM OF CLASSIFICATION AND CODIFICATION

Classification is the basis of business order. Without classification, data, information, and news of business life would be mere fragments, difficult to interpret. Without classification there would be no files, no book-keeping could exist, no one would know what the business owned, what it needed, what it sold. Classification is therefore needed in every business.

If such is the importance of classification, no less great is the importance of codification, which is its necessary complement. The two techniques, in fact, go hand in hand. One seeks out the characteristics which certain phenomena have in common; the other creates them should they be lacking or inadequate to the purpose.

In other words, the problem which classification and codification seek to solve is what name to give to each phenomenon under examination. The systematic grouping of items with similar characteristics comes afterwards and is purely routine work.

A knowledge of the techniques of classification and codification is therefore indispensable for all businesses.

2.3 IDENTIFICATION OF A NAME

We have mentioned identifying the name as the main objective of classification. It is perhaps advisable to point out that *name* in this context is a generic term which includes all distinctive characters which can serve to make up a classification. A name can be selected on the basis of several criteria:

The name of the writer, the addressee, the author, the proprietor or registered owner of that which is being classified.
The name of the item being classified.
The subject dealt with in the document being classified or to which it refers.

The date on which the document being classified was received, mailed or written.

The number given to the item being classified.

Almost each one of the criteria indicated naturally has its corresponding method for putting the material in order. The most common methods, which we shall go into in more detail in later chapters, are:

Alphabetical.
Geographical.
Numerical.
Subject or topic.
Chronological.

Each of the methods indicated can be used either alone or with other methods in a mixed system. We therefore have various classification systems, each with its advantages and disadvantages and each particularly suitable for specific cases.

2.4 CODIFICATION

2.4.1 ALPHABETICAL SYMBOLS

It now seems advisable to delve more deeply into the significance and functions of codification.

Codification can be carried out by using numbers, letters of the alphabet, or a combination of both. In general there seems to be a preference for numbers; letters of the alphabet are seldom used and almost never in cases where complex data-handling equipment is used. For it must not be forgotten that before making a definite choice on the type of code to be used, the type of data-handling equipment to be subsequently used must be taken into consideration. In fact the adapatation of the codes to the technical specifications of the machines is a very delicate question which has to be gone into in depth.

The main advantages of using alphabetical symbols are:

A greater number of headings can be used in a single classification, since there are up to 26 alphabetical symbols against ten numerical ones.

Alphabetical symbols, when appropriately grouped can suggest the name of the item filed, while there can never be any immediate connection between a number and the item filed, except for copy invoices, etc.

Alphabetical coding becomes more inconvenient and difficult to read when very long symbols are required; for this reason alphabetical symbols—assuming they have been taken into consideration—are only used when a few letters are sufficient to identify an item.

Further, it has been observed that more errors take place when alphabetical symbols are used than when numerical ones are.

2.4.2 NUMERICAL SYMBOLS

As opposed to letters, figures can be dealt with more easily and are immediately identifiable when read. Further, figures immediately identify the relative position of two symbols by indicating the number of items which separate them. For instance, it is not immediately obvious that the difference between 'f' and 'p' is the same as that between '6' and '16'.

The greater acceptance which numerical symbols have met with is also due to the fact that many data-handling machines only handle numerical symbols.

2.4.3 ALPHANUMERICAL SYMBOLS

Codes are sometimes made up of a combination of letters and figures, since when a large number of items have to be codified, this method enables the job to be done with much shorter symbols than would be the case if purely numerical symbols were used. Number plates on motor vehicles are a well-known example of mixed coding.

2.5 SIGNIFICANCE OF SYMBOLS

It is obvious that symbols should, if at all possible, be significant, that is, they should clearly and immediately identify the items they represent. However, every code acquires a meaning when the symbols run in some systematic sequence. In other words, items should be arranged in order of size, weight, or frequency of use, according to need.

The following example is quite significant:

Code Number	Description
13000	Electric light bulbs
13020	20 watts
13025	25 watts
13040	40 watts
13060	60 watts
13100	100 watts
13200	200 watts
13250	250 watts

This code is easy to understand because the significant numbers do not need to be interpreted. This method, however, requires a large number of digits, although in the example shown the last three digits could have been reduced to one by numbering each size consecutively.

2.6 BLOCK CODES

There are various types of numerical codes:

1 Codes based on numerical sequence.
2 Block codes.
3 Group codes.
4 Decimal codes.

Codes in (1) and (4) above will be described in detail in chapters 4 and 6 in this part of the book. The other two remain to be examined.

Block codes are set by assigning blocks of numbers in sequence to each category of items to be codified. For instance accounts could be codified as follows:

Code numbers	Description
1–49	a/c receivable
50–79	a/c payable
80–99	net assets

In each block some numbers are left free so that they can be given to items which are added to the classification later on. The number of digits needed in a block code system depends on the number of items to be codified and on the extent of future expansion.

2.7 GROUP CODES

In a group code the digits in the code are arranged in groups or fields, each one of which designates one of the classifications to which the codified item belongs. In this system the digits on the left represent the most important classifications, while the digits which follow from left to right represent the sub-classifications.

Since the position of each digit or group of digits has an exact meaning, the number of digits included in each field must be established in advance. Likewise, the sequence of the various groups must not be altered.

Here is an example of a group code:

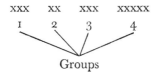

Groups

Such a code could have the following meaning:

Group	Positions	Meaning
1	1–3	Salesman
2	4–5	Branch
3	6–8	Area
4	9–13	Product sold

The code could therefore look like this:

121   05   002   02730

which could mean: salesman 121, at Branch number 5, in area 2, has sold product number 2730 (quantity specified separately).

Group codes are particularly suitable for mechanical data processing because they can easily be extracted and tabulated, whichever classification is used. They are also easy to memorize because of the clear meaning of the figures according to their position. Expansion can be provided for by the provision of temporarily inactive positions.

2.8   THE CLASSIFICATION AND CODIFICATION SYSTEM

From what has been said about classification and codification it becomes obvious that the choice of criteria to be followed must be made according to a system which sets down the principles the classification must follow. The object of the system is to make sure that the classification criteria followed are homogeneous, that the classification is suited to the needs for which it is being made and

C

that the work is being carried out at the lowest possible cost bearing in mind the objectives set.

The system includes one or more of the known techniques, as dictated by the special peculiarities of the business. In order to set up a business classification system it is therefore necessary to:

Define the objectives to be met by the classification.

Know the material to be classified (characteristics, quantity, etc.).

Know the classification techniques.

Obviously it is not possible to determine positively which is the best classification system from a general point of view and which, therefore, is the most advisable *a priori*. Each system is valid within specific situations, which means that a careful and accurate study must be made in each case of the actual needs of the business. Only when the results of this research are known will it be possible to make a satisfactory choice from every point of view.

In any event, when making the choice it is well to bear in mind:

That the system adopted must be simple and give rise to as few doubtful cases to be decided upon by the filing clerk as possible.

It must simplify as much as possible the addition of documents or information and their subsequent retrieval.

It must take into consideration the needs not only of the various existing departments, but also, in so far as possible, of future ones, so that the classification does not have to be altered at a later date.

That the rules laid down must be put into writing, so that they may become formally operative and binding for everyone concerned.

One of the problems most frequently met by someone preparing a classification system is the fact that different offices often request the same document by a different name—one will refer to it by the name on its heading and the other by its number. Undoubtedly, the ideal solution would be for the filing department to be able to comply with both types of request. However, this can sometimes be excessively costly and in such cases it is best to organize the classification according to the most commonly used form of request.

The classification system must also take into consideration the amount of space needed for the filing and the equipment required. In this connection it is sufficient to bear in mind that the degree to which an alphabetical classification can be analysed is influenced by at least four factors:

The quantity of material in the semi-active file.
The number of cross-references.
The average annual increase of material.
The importance of the 'Miscellaneous' folders.

The future increase of filed material can be gauged roughly by carefully examining a number of filing cabinets chosen at random and multiplying the average thickness of the papers by the number of filing cabinets in the office.

As for estimating the amount of space which would be gained by thinning out the older files or estimating future needs, it is best to be extremely cautious and make conservative estimates. Therefore, leave a margin for error in the case of thinning out and give plenty of leeway in estimating future space needs.

Another important topic to be considered is the 'Miscellaneous' section of the files. It is an extremely important section, especially for those companies which have a large number of occasional customers for whom it is not worthwhile having a separate file. In such cases miscellaneous alphabetical positions are established and kept at the end of the alphabet. This is rarely an advisable procedure, because it makes retrieval extremely difficult and is an open invitation to disorder and excessive generality. When a miscellaneous file is absolutely essential, it is advisable for the papers thus preserved to be clearly cross-referenced.

2.9 THE CODIFICATION SYSTEM

Naturally, codes also have to be systematized. Codification systems, which, as mentioned, are part of a broader research into data processing, were previously thought out and developed within the functional area in which they were most frequently used. For instance, materials codes were determined in the production office and accounting codes in the accounts department.

This procedure is no longer viable, since the latest findings in the field of data processing lean more and more towards a reciprocal relationship between codes, since the increasing integration of the processing operations also poses the problem of integrating codes. All those responsible for the running of the business must therefore co-operate in the establishment of the codes and since every code almost always has some connection with the accounting department, it is advisable to entrust the top administrative executive with the task of co-ordinating this work and revising the codes.

When codes are not determined in such a spirit of co-operation, it frequently happens that items identified by different symbols are, in effect, identical. The elimination of duplications makes it possible automatically to reduce the number of items to be codified and opens the way to savings, which sometimes can be quite considerable. It can bring about a reduction in the number of items in the stores, book-keeping entries, etc.

As the various items are being identified a description should be made of each one, in order to clarify the results on the preliminary research. These descriptions will be the point of departure for future reference, should doubts arise as to the classification of the items within the group.

The terminology used in these descriptions should be standardized. It would be advisable to bear this warning constantly in mind.

As for general rules to be followed in classifying the codified items, the following can be said:

Items should be classified one at a time.

Overlappings must be avoided and each item must be filed under one classification only.

A place must be allotted for each item within the group. Where a small number of items is involved a mixed classification can be used, so long as separate groups are not justified by the quantity of the items.

For those who wish to follow up this subject in more depth, reference should be made to *Commodity Coding*, published by the National Computing Centre Limited (1968), plus HMSO and BSI publications on these subjects.

3
CLASSIFICATION BY NAME IN ALPHABETICAL ORDER

3.1 DEFINITION

In classification by name in alphabetical order the material is identified by the heading on the document, form, letter or other material and is filed in sequential alphabetical order, much as the telephone directory lists the names of subscribers.

Classification by name in alphabetical order is the basis of many filing systems, and in a way it is the simplest of all classification techniques, but in practice it involves many problems and difficulties which are not obvious to the uninitiated.

This classification technique is the most common and it is estimated that it is used in at least 85% of filing departments. Its wide use can be explained by the fact that alphabetical order does not rule out the use of other classification techniques, which can in fact complement one another. If, for instance, material is filed in geographical order or in subject order, the items within each category can be filed in alphabetical order.

3.2 ADVANTAGES AND DISADVANTAGES

The advantages of classification by name in alphabetical order are the following:

1 Simplicity of the classification system: there is no need for classes, sub-classes or other sub-divisions and the only knowledge needed to classify the material is the name of the classified items or of the company or person to whom the document refers. The preliminary filing work is therefore reduced to the absolute minimum, with consequent saving of time.

2 Familiarity with the method: alphabetical order is one of the most traditional and it is familiar to everyone from school days. So long as the material to be classified contains no special difficulties, this method will require a minimum of staff training and will not suffer if staff has to be changed.

3 Elasticity: it is always possible to insert new names in exactly the right place.

4 Low cost: the material can be filed in simple inexpensive cabinets.

5 Simplicity of retrieval: any document can easily be located, consulted and replaced, without the need to look up filing plans, reference tables, etc.

On the other hand classification by name in alphabetical order has the following disadvantages:

1 The filing criteria are not foolproof: it is easy for doubts to arise, for errors to be made and for those doing the filing and those retrieving a document to follow different criteria. For instance, some people would file a letter from De La Rue Bull Machines under 'De', while someone else may look for it under 'Bull'. Similarly, some people might file a letter from Joseph Lucas under 'Joseph', while others might file it under 'Lucas'.

2 If there is a great deal of material, well-trained staff is needed: in order to avoid errors very detailed rules must be set down and they can only be followed with accuracy by well-trained staff. Further, the rules alone are not sufficient to remove all doubts, and uncertainties can still easily arise, followed by contradictions, errors and loss of time.

3 The more material there is, the greater is the incidence of identical names. For instance, how many Joseph Smiths are there in Britain? Obviously, in an alphabetical classification by name no error could more easily be made than to file the correspondence from Joseph Smith of Bath in the folder for Joseph Smith of Coventry.

4 Frequently, further elaboration is very difficult. Imagine, for instance, a card-index system containing the names of 7000 customers in alphabetical order. It would not be possible to check how many customers there are in each area, how many orders have come from each area, etc. unless the whole file were reorganized.

In conclusion, classification by name in alphabetical order is to be recommended as the only system when the material to be filed is not very copious, when the possibilities of error are limited and when the adoption of this method results in considerable flexibility. It is therefore ideal for small files and card-indexes and for small libraries which it is not planned to expand very much. If the opposite is the case, then considerable empty space must be left empty in cabinets, cupboards, files, etc. to allow for expansion. In addition, it is necessary for the name of the material to be filed to be known already or easy to ascertain. In the previous chapter the disadvantages of alphabetic codification were listed and it is therefore unnecessary to reiterate the fact that if a name is not readily available, it is best to fall back on other systems.

For the reasons given this classification technique is usually only used for correspondence, libraries, reading rooms, and reference books. Only in exceptional cases is it used for other material.

In the following sections we shall therefore limit ourselves to examining how this technique has to be used in filing correspondence, cards or similar documents.

3.3 PRINCIPLES OF CLASSIFICATION

3.3.1 PREMISE

The efficiency of classification by name in alphabetical order depends on the establishment of rules for handling doubtful cases and to make the work uniform throughout.

Apart from a few exceptions, there are no hard and fast rules, universally adopted, for classification in alphabetical order. The experience of large businesses has, however, enabled some practical guide-lines to be laid down, which can usefully be followed in conjunction with others suited to the particular case, with the aim of facilitating filing and retrieval, reducing doubts to a minimum, and avoiding subjective interpretations which result in several files being opened for the same name.

3.3.2 NAMES OF PEOPLE

The names of individual people recur with great frequency in classifications by name in alphabetical order. They are easier to file if it is borne in mind that it is necessary to:

Write on the material—if it is not already on it—first the surname, then the title, if any, followed by the given name. If this information is already printed on the document, then all that is needed is to underline the surname.

File the surnames according to the exact sequence of the letters which make them up. If there are several identical surnames, the material is filed according to the given name, i.e. first Smith Arthur, then Smith Bernard, followed by Smith Charles. The same rule applies to names of activities. For instance, first you will have Gas, then Gas (Bottlers), the latter being simply a category within the main subject.

Fuse together into a single word all surnames beginning with a prefix. For filing purposes De Havilland becomes Dehavilland. The same applies to foreign surnames.

Avoid any abbreviation which may give rise to errors. For this reason Brown Sara must not become Brown S.

Add any indication necessary for the exact identification of the person concerned, after the surname, title and given name. If necessary junior and senior can also be added.

3.3.3. NAMES OF FIRMS

It is extremely important for correct classification to establish exact rules with regard to the names of companies, organizations, associations and so on. Such names are, in effect, harder to file, particularly in view of the fact that it is not advisable, apart from a few exceptional cases, to go by their exact legal name. Outside of official documents a company's name gets shortened or otherwise altered and this popular version becomes current and replaces, to all intents and purposes, the company's full legal name.

The main rules to follow are the following:

1 The name of a company is always more important than one of its departments or department heads. A letter signed by John Brown, Sales Manager, Sales Division, Alpha Company should not be filed under Brown John, nor yet under Sales Division, but under Alpha Company. In the case of large companies, however, the appropriate divisions can be as follows:

DUNLOP Tyre and Rubber Company Ltd.—
Purchasing Division
DUNLOP Tyre and Rubber Company Ltd.—
Flooring Sales Division

2 When a company's name is made up of a name and surname, it is advisable, for filing purposes to invert the order, i.e. Rudolph Lang must be filed under Lang Rudolph and William H. Smith under Smith William H. and so on.

3 Company names preceded by an indication of the activity they carry out must also be inverted for filing purposes, e.g. Restaurant Bourguignonne should be filed under Bourguignonne Restaurant.

4 When the name of a company comprises the given names of two brothers followed by the surname, it is advisable to repeat the surname after each name in order to avoid confusion. Joseph and Anthony Brown will consequently be filed as Brown Joseph (and) Brown Anthony. If the surname were not repeated the two given names might appear to belong to the same person.

5 For filing purposes the article 'The' must be ignored. For instance, The Bell Company should be filed under Bell Company (The). Prepositions and other small words are likewise ignored. Institute for the Blind should be filed as Institute (for the) Blind.

6 'And' or '&' should likewise be ignored as far as filing is concerned. Ronalds & White should be filed as Ronalds (&) White, ignoring the ampersand altogether.

7 When a legal name includes figures, they should be read as if written out, e.g. 7th Commission for Civic Affairs becomes Seventh Commission for Civic Affairs and is filed accordingly.

8 In order to avoid errors all abbreviations are discouraged. The one exception is a company known by its initials. In such cases it is advisable to file according to the initials, perhaps with a cross-reference under the full name, e.g. FIAT (Fabbrica Italiana Automobili Torino) would go under FIAT, perhaps with a cross-reference under Fabbrica Italiana Automobili Torino. This exception is justified, since documents not written on official company stationery are frequently made out using initials only, rather than the full company name. Time would

inevitably be wasted if such material were filed under the company's full name, many such companies being generally known by their initials. IBM is another example of such a case.

9 In the case of identical names, it is best to put the towns where the company operates in alphabetical order, e.g.

Barclays Bank Limited, Brighton.
Barclays Bank Limited, London.
Barclays Bank Limited, Oxford.

10 When there are a great many names to file, it is advisable to ignore those words with which a number of company or organization names begin. This overcomes the disadvantages of having an excessively large group of names with the same first word. Such words are: Consulate, Association, School, etc. Consulate General of Peru, would be filed under Peru, Consulate General.

11 Distributors, commission agents and the like who act on behalf of their principals must be filed under the principal's name, e.g. George and James Black, Ford Distributors must be filed under Ford, perhaps with a subsidiary file for Distributors. In any event there will have to be a cross-reference under Black George (and) Black James.

The above eleven classification rules have been set out in Table 3.1.

Table 3.1 RECAPITULATION OF PRINCIPLES OF CLASSIFICATION IN ALPHABETICAL ORDER OF COMPANIES, ORGANIZATIONS AND ASSOCIATIONS

Name	1st classification guide	2nd classification guide	3rd classification, guide
Fredrick Brown & Co.	Brown	Fredrick	(&) Co.
Barclays Bank Ltd.	Barclays	Bank Ltd.	Brighton, London, Oxford
Foreign Exchange Depart-ment, Barclays Bank Ltd.	Barclays	Bank Ltd.	Foreign Exchange Department
IBM United Kingdom Ltd.[1]	IBM	United Kingdom Ltd.	
Restaurant Bourguignonne	Bourguignonne	Restaurant	
George and James Black,[2] Ford Distributors	Ford	Distributors	Black George (and) Black James

[1] Insert a cross-reference under International Business Machines
[2] Insert a cross-reference under George Black and James Black

3.3.4   GEOGRAPHICAL NAMES AND FOREIGN WORDS

Particular care must be taken when classifying geographical terms and foreign words. We suggest the following rules:

1 Geographical names composed of more than one word are most commonly filed by considering each word as a separate entity. This method is not the most rational, however, since it is much easier to file a name if it consists of one word only. Here are some examples:

The separate unit way	*The single word way*
Morton in Marsh	Mortoninmarsh
Ashby de la Zouche	Ashbydelazouche
Harrow on the Hill	Harrowonthehill
Upton Upon Severn	Uptonuponsevern

2 Names beginning with St (abbreviation of Saint) should be filed as if written out in full, e.g. St Martin's in the Field should be filed as if written Saint Martin's in the Field.

3 If the name of a city is preceded by an article, the latter should be joined to the name, e.g. The Hague is filed under Thehague, not Hague (The).

4 Foreign words should be filed according to the sequence of letters, not according to pronunciation. When there are two ways of writing a word (such as German words with an umlaut), a cross-reference should be made, e.g. Müller, see Mueller.

5 Certain descriptions which sometimes precede names should follow them for filing purposes, e.g.

Canada Dominion (of), not Dominion of Canada.

San Marino Republic (of), not Republic of San Marino.

3.4 CLASSIFICATION WITHIN INDIVIDUAL FILES

The principles given are general ones and must from time to time be adapted to specific situations. It must not be forgotten, however, that they are not abstract rules, but aim at facilitating both the filing and the retrieval of material, reducing to a minimum the number of possible doubts and cutting down on the cases in which it is necessary to look into a number of files to find what one is looking for or several files are opened for the same name.

As for filing the individual papers within a single folder, the orders most frequently used are the following:

CHRONOLOGICAL (usually the latest date on top and the oldest at the bottom. This order is suitable when the papers in every individual file are not very numerous, when they do not have to be consulted very frequently and when they do not have to be divided into subject matter.

BY SUBJECT MATTER. This order is useful when it is necessary to facilitate the consultation of material on a given subject. This order is not used very much, since frequently the same paper refers to a number of subjects.

MIXED. Some of the documents are classified by subject matter and some in chronological order. An instance of this would be to have three folders, one containing all the correspondence in date order, the second containing all invoices, likewise in date order, and the third containing all delivery notes in date order.

4
CLASSIFICATION BY NAME IN NUMERICAL ORDER

4.1 DEFINITION

In classification by name in numerical order the material is collected and sorted according to a name which in this particular circumstance takes the form of a progressive number. The numbering can be consecutive, as in the case of invoices or can follow special criteria, as we shall see further on.

Classification by name in numerical order differs from codification by number mentioned in chapter 2 by the simple fact that ordering the files on a number basis does not in this case permit the numbers to identify exactly the content of the documents classified.

4.2 ADVANTAGES AND DISADVANTAGES

The advantages of classification in numerical order can be summarized as follows:

1 It is always possible to assign an identification number to material, while it is often difficult to give it a name.
2 Numbers permit the material to be identified in the most precise possible way. When classifying the material by name in alphabetical order its designation may be incomplete (for instance one may know only the surname and initial or, in the case of a woman, only her maiden name, etc.). In classifying it by number, on the other hand, unless a transcription error is made, it is always complete and it is impossible to confuse it with another or not to recognize it.
3 Numbers are more easily read than letters. It is easier to read 334.479 than Smith Joseph, 24 Hill Crescent, Brighton, Sussex.

This makes the classification work faster and more accurate as well as the filing and retrieval.

4 In ordering numbers there can be no doubt as to where to put them. In classifying names in alphabetical order there can be a multitude of reasons for uncertainty and as many possibilities of error. This is not the case with numbers, each of which has its own definite place. The only difficulties which can arise are those resulting from faulty writing or interpretation of the numbers.

5 Numbers are a form of identification which makes it much easier to insert and retrieve the material at the classification stage. As we shall see in more detail further on, material is classified by stages, dividing it each time in six to ten groups. This work is much easier with numbers than with letters. For instance, if 10 000 documents numbered from 1 to 10 000 are to be classified, first they will be divided into groups from 1 to 999, 1000 to 1999, 2000 to 2999 and so on. Then the first group will be taken (1 to 999) and it will be divided into hundreds; next the 1 to 99 group will be divided into tens and finally each of the tens will be put in sequences. It is far more difficult to do the same work with letters.

6 Classifying material in numerical order does not require skilled staff if the material is already numbered.

On the other hand, classification in numerical order has a serious disadvantage: it is impossible to retrieve the material unless the number under which it is filed is known or unless the numerical order coincides with the alphabetical or geographical one. This means that every time something is classified in numerical order it is necessary to keep a code or guide for the location of individual files (but see section 13.6), and this nullifies many of the advantages of this system.

It should also be borne in mind that it is often advisable to do the numbering in blocks so that new numbers can be inserted (this happens when the numerical order coincides with the alphabetical or geographical one). The blocks can go in tens, hundreds or thousands according to how many fresh numbers may have to be added. It follows that very high numbers with seven or eight digits can be reached. Further, in spite of this precaution, it often happens that all free numbers are taken up and sub-classifications have to be resorted to, e.g. 100/1, 100/2.

After a time, it can become difficult to keep up progressive numbering and alphabetical or geographic order and the classification becomes confused and full of complex numbers. The possibilities of error are increased and the whole numbering has to be done again.

Finally, it is easy to make errors in the reading or transcribing of the numbers and in such cases the consequences are more serious than is the case for identical errors made in reading or transcribing names.

4.3 USES OF NUMERICAL CLASSIFICATION

For the reasons given, classification in numerical order is only to be used in specific cases. It has in fact been completely abandoned for ordinary correspondence, but is still used, in conjunction with other systems, for some types of documents, orders, e.g. invoices, or delivery and despatch notes.

We mention a combination with other systems because it often happens that orders and invoices, especially, are classified in progressive numerical order (one copy) and alphabetically in the customer's or supplier's file (the second copy). In this way, the copy in numerical order is of use only to those concerned with the object of the order or the invoice and they pay no attention to the name of the customer or the supplier. This is the case in accounting and statistical departments, for instance.

The numerical system is also suitable for law offices, hospital administration, and insurance companies which, as a rule, have to keep documents for a much longer period than commercial offices.

One disadvantage is that it does not allow for a 'Miscellaneous' file and it is therefore necessary to open a file and allot a number even for a single paper. If a law office is working on a number of different cases for the same client, all the necessary cross-references must be given on the appropriate cards.

Finally, numerical classification is indicated in cases where you want to be certain that no material will get lost. By numbering every document in sequence without omitting any number it is possible to ascertain at any moment if something is missing.

The adoption of classification in numerical order can also be justified on the grounds of privacy. For instance, in the case of patents or formulae it is frequently advisable not to have the various elements which distinguish them on view in the files.

In other circumstances this method is advisable for reasons of organization. Insurance companies are an instance of such a case. They allot a number to each of their contracts and ask their clients to quote this number in the case of claims, payments, etc., thus avoiding the necessity of referring to their code book.

4.4 TRANSPOSITIONS

Although classification in numerical order is among the simplest both to organize and as an exercise, a great deal of attention has to be given to the work in order to avoid possible mental transposition of the digits.

It is easy absentmindedly to read number 269.241 as 269.214 and to file it in the latter file. The gravity of such a simple mistake

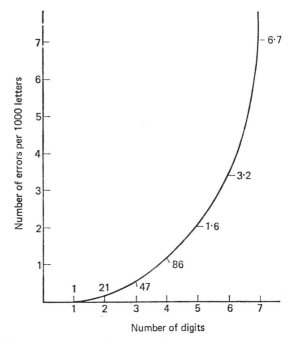

Fig. 4.1 Graph showing the increase in the number of errors as the number of digits increases

is obvious, since it would be extremely difficult to retrace a document misfiled in this way.

The only remedy for such a drawback, which is unfortunately quite frequent, is to make periodical checks of the individual files and this work considerably increases the cost of running the filing system.

This transposition problem becomes even more serious if it is borne in mind that its frequency increases in geometric proportion to the number of digits which a number contains, as shown in Fig. 4.1.

4.5 THE TERMINAL FIGURE SYSTEM

A great deal of research has been carried out by experts on the problem of reducing the probability of making transposition errors. One of the most satisfactory solutions to this problem is offered by the terminal figure system. This consists in dividing the distinctive numbers of the various positions in two or three groups which are read from right to left.

If, for instance, a card belonging to Mr Brown Charles is given number 4489943, this number can be broken down into the following three groups: 448.99.43 to be read in the following sequence: 43.99.448. No. 43 is therefore called primary, No. 99 secondary and number 448 final.

In the card box the cards must be separated by indicators (Fig. 4.2). Those on the right indicate all the primary groups, that is, in the example given, all cards ending with 43, while the central indicators mark all secondary groups, that is in our example, all cards ending in 9943.

This simple expedient considerably reduces the number of filing errors because it diminishes the number of digits which the filing clerk has to remember. Instead of having to remember a six-digit number, only two or three numbers each containing two or three digits have to be borne in mind. While it is true that the filing clerk will have to repeat his remembering effort for as many times as there are isolated groups, the total number of errors will nonetheless be reduced, in view of the geometric progression of their frequency (Fig. 4.1). To quote but a single example, if we reckon that every 2000 operations dealing with three-digit numbers (1000 six-digit numbers subdivided into three-digit groups) should produce one

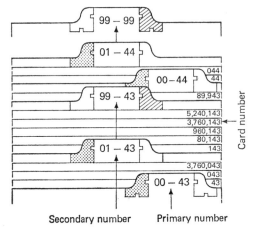

Fig. 4.2   The terminal figure system

mistake, according to the graph, 1000 six-digit numbers would probably produce three mistakes.

While a 3% error rate may appear to be minimal, it appears far more significant if it is borne in mind that one filing error can cost between £20 and £50, sometimes even more.

The terminal figure system also permits a very rapid check of erroneously filed cards (see Fig. 4.2). In addition it facilitates the final filing stage, since the classification of the material is far more rapid.

4.6   COLOURS

Another system which reduces errors in filing material which has been classified in numerical order is the use of colours. The system consists in allotting a different colour to every digit from 0 to 9. In order to do this it is necessary to have ten files, each in a different colour and appropriately numbered in which to file the documents.

Although there are many opinions on the subject, it is usual to associate the colour with the penultimate digit, indicating the tens. This selection stems from the observation that when a reading error is made it is almost always made in the last three digits.

Figure 4.3, which shows the incidence of errors in relation to the position of the digits, makes it clear that if colour is associated with the penultimate digit, the result will be a considerable reduction in the number of errors in an area in which they very frequently occur. Since the penultimate digit controls transpositions of the last and third before last digits, it is much more important in checking such mistakes than the last digit, even though this is more frequently transposed.

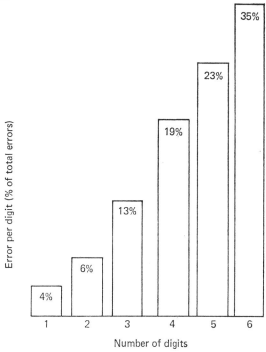

Fig. 4.3 Chart showing frequency of error with position of digit

Obviously, however, regardless of the digit–colour link used, the mis-filing of a folder can be spotted immediately by the filing clerk, since a folder of a given colour would be filed with a group of folders of a different colour. In other words, in order to make an error, the filing clerk would actually have to make two: first he would have to mis-read the number, then he would have to file a folder of one colour with folders of a different colour.

As for the choice of colours, it is well to bear in mind that:

The colours should be easily distinguishable one from the other. Similar colours must be associated with numbers that are rarely confused.

The tone of the colours must be such as to cause no confusion to partially colour-blind filing clerks.

It is not at all necessary for the files to be completely coloured, in fact it has been noted that the colours are much more effective when limited to a longitudinal stripe and if each colour has its own position.

Finally, it should be pointed out that the distinctive number of each folder should be placed, by preference, in the top right-hand corner, using a rubber stamp or an automatic numbering device.

4.7 OTHER REMARKS

The use of colours is indicated above all in avoiding errors in placing files in their proper places in drawers and cabinets. To avoid retrieval errors it is advisable for the filing clerk to know not only the number of the file but the name the material in it refers to. In this way it is possible to check right away what has been found against what is being looked for.

Several companies use a numerical classification for filing customer cards according to their salesmen's itineraries or calls by service personnel, etc. In such cases the order in which calls must be made is first established by appropriate techniques and then customers assigned to each salesman are given a progressive number, usually ten by ten or 100 by 100 in order to permit the inclusion of new names. The numbers are then transferred to the cards, which are filed in consecutive order.

In some companies the customer's distinguishing number is made up of several sections and thereby becomes a code. The first section indicates the area, the second the name of the salesman covering the area, the third the itinerary, and the fourth the order in which the customer must be called upon.

Usually such a system is advisable if the person making the call uses the cards himself. Otherwise, checking and especially keeping the cards up to date becomes extremely complex.

If this classification system is adopted, it is advisable to make use of maps, plans and street maps in conjunction with it. Any doubts can then be resolved without difficulty. In some cases, the customer's location is actually marked on the card by means of appropriate symbols.

Classification in numerical order does not require any special equipment and can be carried out equally well in a filing cabinet, suspended files or card-indexes.

The only complication which this method entails is that it is almost always necessary to keep an index permitting the speedy identification of the material concealed behind each number.

5

CLASSIFICATION BY NAME IN GEOGRAPHICAL ORDER

5.1 DEFINITION

The filing of documents in geographical order has much to commend it in certain types of business or in certain circumstances in general businesses, but it is normally used for filing customer correspondence or lists of addresses according to the residence of the correspondent.

Import and export businesses, mail-order and direct-mail companies, publishers, particularly those with overseas or regional correspondents, and wholesale businesses might find it advantageous to file by geographic area, or by grouping for a particular purpose.

This purpose could be the supply of commodities, product locations such as oil, wood, coal, steel, etc., by area and then by name of supplier. Or it could be religious or political growth or even location by language for purposes of market research or the printing of sales literature and so on.

5.2 SYSTEMS

There are two main types of system used:

A location name guide which can be by country, then county, town and street, or alternatively for localised requirements just a town with suppliers or correspondents' names in alphabetical order.

A straight alphabetic listing with lettered guides and a number for each file. For world-wide filing by country this could be Aden, file A1; Afghanistan, file A2; Albania, file A3, Algeria, file A4, etc.

There are, of course, variations on these basic patterns according to each company's individual requirements.

It might be more useful to file by geographic areas, say Northern Europe, Central Europe, Eastern Europe and Southern Europe, and then file by the person or correspondent in that area.

For more localized filing, say in the United Kingdom, this could be divided into County, Town and Company. Or for local Government filing into County Boroughs, Rural District, Urban District, or allocation by street or electoral register.

It may be that the name of a large town, divided into regions will provide a better geographical division to suit a particular system.

Alternative groupings can be made, but for easy filing a full alphabetic index cross-referenced to the geographic location may be necessary to avoid mis-filing.

5.3 ADVANTAGES AND DISADVANTAGES

The advantage of this type of filing is obvious to certain types of businesses already mentioned, that it classifies the material into readily identifiable groups and could be used to make a check on representatives in a certain area or region to estimate sales or commission.

Or this could be used as a basis for deciding on the volume of sales in each area as to whether a new representative should be appointed or a new branch opened, etc.

In the case of direct-mailing or mail-order companies, a geographic breakdown will indicate certain areas which should be mailed for seasonal goods and so on. The applications in your own business will probably be as obvious.

There are, however, certain disadvantages which should not be overlooked.

The staff responsible for filing must have more than a working knowledge of geography, or must be taught it.

Where there are names of individuals in each area, these must be linked by a cross-index to the main geographic filing; should an individual move, or write from a different address, it must be ascertained if this move is temporary or permanent and whether the file location should be changed, or the individual file re-allocated to a new area.

If for any reason a different classification is required, then the whole of the geographic filing pattern may need re-arranging and addresses re-writing. Further, if for any reason a company cannot operate in a certain area, or has traded there but is not trading at present, space must be left for future requirements which may be difficult to estimate.

It is not flexible if products or subjects are variable from various areas and it can lead to difficulties by name similiarities in different areas.

For instance in Britain there is a town of Abingdon in Berkshire and an Abingdon in Lanarkshire. There is an Ashford in Kent and an Ashfordby in Leicestershire, although this is also spelt 'Asfordby'. In Eire there is Ballycastle in County Mayo and a Ballycastle in Antrim, Northern Ireland, and there is a River Avon in four different counties of Hampshire, Wiltshire, Warwickshire and Banffshire, Scotland.

This perhaps illustrates the need for care in filing and clarity of addressing.

5.4   CLASSIFICATION BY COUNTY

For filing in Britain it is advantageous to file by county, although it must be remembered that in other countries it is different. In the United States, filing could be by states. In Italy by region and province. In Switzerland by canton. It must be decided whether the advantage of fractionalising files to this extent outweighs any disadvantages.

Filing in county order, then the name of the largest towns in the county and by name of individual or company may be a sufficiently diverse breakdown.

There are, however, problems with large towns such as London, Birmingham, Manchester and so on which have postal areas of say, W 14, SW 1, NW 1, etc., which have similarities in suffix but are widely separated in area. Also if an area name is given it is necessary to know that Southwark is London SE 1, but so is Bermondsey and some parts of Vauxhall are also SE 1. Also parts of Bermondsey might be SE 1 or SE 16, according to its location. Similarly SW 1 can contain Chelsea, Knightsbridge and Victoria.

5.5   CLASSIFICATION BY TOWN

Therefore, a town classification with the county name to follow might be a more advantageous breakdown in some cases, such as

Abberley, Worcestershire; Aber, Caernarvon; Aberavon, Cardigan; Aberdare, Glamorganshire; and so on.

The large town could be broken down into areas in alphabetical order such as Hampstead NW 3, Hendon NW 4, Homerton E 9, or numerical order NW 3 Hampstead, NW 4 Hendon, NW 5 Kentish Town and so on, depending on how the documents were likely to be addressed and the type of reference required.

5.6 CLASSIFICATION BY STREET IN A TOWN

There are occasions where some companies, such as those who carry out door-to-door selling or advertising campaigns who might find it advantageous to file by street name in a particular town.

This would give them a ready-made reference to numbers of houses approached, kind of sales achieved, class of street and occupants, etc.

There are a number of other occasions for small traders where such a breakdown may have advantages over other geographic filing.

The new postal codes being used by the GPO will also have the effect of isolating streets or areas of a town and in some cases individual buildings or companies.

For instance, the local area to be coded is known as a 'machine town'. This is designated by two letters and in the case of a large town such as Croydon would be CR, or Leeds as LS, but in the case of London might be only W 1 (initials W1) as the 'machine town'.

Following that would be one figure and then a second block of one figure and two letters which would be the 'postman's walk' and the particular streets or firms.

Typical coding would appear as CR1 1AH, or CR7 5OR, etc.

In Croydon for instance over 800 firms have been allocated individual code numbers and in all about 7000 individual codes have been allocated to speed up the post office sorting process.

This type of classification is not yet available for every town but could be used to advantage when it becomes more widely used on a national scale.

5.7 CLASSIFICATION BY HOUSE NUMBER IN AREAS

There are a few occasions such as in municipal or government filing, and occasionally in commercial, where the number of a house or flat,

followed by the street name should be grouped in areas. This is useful for card indexes in small or rural areas where the electoral register is kept in this manner, or rating valuations on property do not require to be filed under the tenant's name.

5.8   CLASSIFICATION WITHIN INDIVIDUAL FILES: NUMERIC

The breakdown of individual files in each of the various geographic groupings is again a matter for individual consideration.

The method of a numerical breakdown for countries, A1, A2, A3, etc. has already been mentioned and this could be taken further.

For instance Britain, which in a world classification might be numbered B6, could have individual towns as a stroke number. Birmingham could be B6/1, Brighton B6/2, Cambridge B6/3 and so on.

The problem which arises here and will arise for almost every country/town breakdown by number will be that an alphabetic cross-reference will be needed. For instance in the above case it may be necessary to add Bournemouth to the listings at a later date, but this might become B6/37 or some such number which would not indicate that alphabetically it came between Birmingham and Brighton.

Another problem is whether to break Britain down into England, Wales, Scotland and Northern Ireland for classification before numbering. This will depend on your need for this kind of differentiation.

An alternative is to list companies or individuals by number classification in geographic areas, but again this needs careful indexing on card or strip indexes with space to insert alphabetic cross references where needed.

5.9   CLASSIFICATION WITHIN INDIVIDUAL FILES: DEWEY SYSTEM

In libraries and in large companies where subject and area are often just as important as each other, the Dewey Decimal System, or modified versions of it are used.

Dewey uses area tables in conjunction with the main subject index (see chapter 6). In this, cultural processes would be in subject index

as 301.29, but cultural processes in Japan (with Japan as –52 in the geographic table) would be 301.295 2, i.e. 52 simply added on to the main subject classification.

The actual classification used, as a suffix where necessary, is as follows:

1 Region.
2 Person.
3 Ancient World.
4–9 Modern World.

This is sub-divided roughly as follows:

41 Scotland and Ireland.
411–414 Divisions of Scotland.
416–419 Divisions of Ireland.
42 British Isles.
421 Greater London, including outer ring and Middlesex.
422 Southeast England (Surrey, Kent, Sussex, Hants, Berks, Isle of Wight), and so on.

43 Central Europe.
44 France.
45 Italy, 453 might be Venice, Italy.
5 is Asia.
6 Africa.
7 North America.
8 South America.
9 Other parts of the world.

So reverting back to section 5.8, numeric classification by the Dewey System for Birmingham might be 424.32, but for Brighton it would be 422.78 or similar, as the Dewey classification is by region, starting with London, proceeding south and west then swinging north to return to finish in Wales. The American inventor separated Scotland and Ireland with separate numbers.

So it has the disadvantage for ordinary staff that it requires a knowledge of British (or world) geography to file by town or even county names.

5.10 MIXED LISTING

The alternative is an alphabetic listing of companies or individuals, or even by subject under a general geographic listing, but each of these suffers from some of the disadvantages ascribed to each method already explained as well as in part some of the geographic disadvantages, but might in certain cases be the correct method to adopt.

6
CLASSIFICATION BY SUBJECT MATTER AND CATEGORY (OR CLASS)

6.1 DEFINITION

Classification by subject matter implies grouping the material according to the subject matter (or a subject matter) which characterizes it, 'subject' meaning a certain characteristic of the material which it is felt should be given special prominence.

A classic example of classification by subject matter are libraries which usually organize their books according to the subjects they deal with. Naturally the types of subject classification which a library can adopt are almost infinite, since every book can contain references to various subjects.

This type of classification therefore requires that an expert in the method adopted arrange the material beforehand by indicating under which subject matter the classification should be made, by using procedures which vary from case to case.

Once the material has been divided by subject matter, it can be further divided according to various criteria, the principal ones being:

1 In alphabetical order according to subject.

2 The grouping of subjects according to logical categories, according to one of the following criteria:

a *Numerical* Each main subject is given a number and the various sub-subjects are likewise given a number which is added to the first one.

b *Alphanumerical* Each main subject is given a number or a letter, while sub-subjects are given a letter or a number, which is added to the first.

c *Decimal* Based on the Dewey system.

A typical example of classification by subject matter, with a grouping of the subjects according to logical categories, is the book-keeping system.

6.2   ADVANTAGES AND DISADVANTAGES

Classification by subject matter is the only one permitting the material to be ordered according to its content. Whatever its limitations, drawbacks and difficulties, it is obvious that, because of its characteristics, it is necessary to fall back on this technique in the following cases:

1 When it is necessary to collect and file material from research and development offices, secretariats, libraries, statistical and book-keeping offices, etc. Classification by subject matter is also necessary when collecting general information on certain products, manufacturing procedures, sales in a given area, etc. The same applies to card-indexes in libraries and for purchasing offices that may need to divide their list of suppliers not alphabetically according to their names, but according to the material they supply.

2 When an individual file contains a great deal of material of different content and value, it may be advisable to divide it into subject matter (we have already mentioned this possibility in connection with alphabetical classification). A file belonging to a given customer could be subdivided into the following groups:
General correspondence
Contracts
Invoices and debit and credit notes
Offers
Material delivered
Requests or other correspondence connected with the fulfilment of contracts.
This system can also be adopted for filing internal memoranda, which can sometimes be quite voluminous. The important thing is judiciously to select the various subjects into which the material is to be divided.

3 When there is a need to keep certain material handy. For instances, files labelled 'Taxes', 'Contributions', 'Pending', 'Complaints', 'Unpaid Bills' can be opened to keep such important matters constantly in evidence.

Generally speaking, it can be said that classification by subject matter is in use in every business, since the files are never organized in a single way, but are divided into broad categories (subjects) and then, within these subjects, according to particular criteria. It is relatively easy, and in many cases convenient, to separate, for instance, customer correspondence from supplier correspondence and from correspondence with dealers. It is obvious, however, that, gradually, once a certain stage is reached, greater and greater difficulties are encountered and these, as can be deduced from what has been previously written, stem from:

The difficulty in deciding under what heading to file a given paper.

The possibility that a given paper may fit into more than one heading.

The high degree of skill needed by the filing staff in deciding under which headings the material belongs.

The high number of possible errors which can be made in assigning the right headings. While it is perfectly possible for two people to agree on how headings should be given, in time even the same person tends to vary the reasoning behind the classification decided upon.

The difficulty in finding the material filed, since in order to retrieve a paper it is necessary to know exactly what principles have been followed in filing it.

The considerable cost of such a classification system, due to the complexity of the procedures to be followed, the qualifications of the staff employed and the time required.

To these general difficulties must be added those inherent in the classification system adopted.

The analysis of the advantages and disadvantages of the technique under discussion will be completed as the various criteria are considered.

6.3 ALPHABETICAL CLASSIFICATION BY SUBJECT MATTER

This is the most popular technique since it permits the insertion of new items without difficulty, avoids the complex problem of grouping the subjects into categories—such groups are never perfect and compromises always have to be made—and retrieval requires no special training.

In this case also, and indeed in every form of classification by subject matter, the difficulty is represented by the choice of subjects, which must express the concept of a given topic in the clearest and most inclusive way possible, preferably in a single word. This word must be in the plural, unless custom or other considerations suggest the singular.

In studying this classification system, it is important to define the degree of analysis which it is desired to reach. If the headings (subjects) cover too broad a content, many of the advantages of the classification by subject matter can be lost, but on the other hand the material will be easier to sort and frequently also to retrieve. Conversely, if too fine an analysis is aimed at, there may be classification problems and retrieval may become more difficult.

In general, the extent to which the material is broken down should therefore depend on the characteristics of the material to be classified and the reasons for which the classification is being carried out.

In some cases, very broad headings are given to start with. These are then broken down into sub-headings, which are sub-divided once again. This method is called 'encyclopaedic'. The headings are put into alphabetical order, the sub-headings likewise, and the sub-sub-headings in turn.

In order to facilitate classification and consultation, heading, sub-heading and sub-sub-heading are all shown on the document, usually written in a different way, and separated by a dash or underlined in a different colour. Sometimes the sub-sub-headings are not put into alphabetical order under the sub-heading to which they refer, but are merely annotated to facilitate consultation.

Whatever the method adopted, the degree of analysis must be decided upon according to logical rules, without ever going into details of scant use. For instance the following breakdown is erroneous:

Tables
—Oak
—Metal
—Office

since each of the sub-divisions can in turn be broken down from a different angle. An exact breakdown of the subject 'Tables' could be the following:

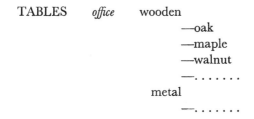

In selecting the various topics, the person working out the classification should consult the various technical offices concerned and, if necessary, an expert librarian.

If any doubt should remain, the final decision should rest with the person responsible for the classification, since only he is in a position to examine all the material from the same point of view.

It frequently happens that the same material could be classified under several headings. In such a case criteria must be established to decide which heading the material is to be placed under, unless it is possible to secure several copies of the material in question.

The headings and descriptions of the contents (objects) can be deceptive. For instance, a file headed 'Rules for the Prevention of Accidents' certainly cannot be classified under 'Rules', but under 'Accidents', 'Prevention of Accidents', or similar headings according to the type of classification adopted.

When the same subject can be designated in several ways, it is advisable to make use of cross-references, which usually are particularly numerous in classifications by subject matter in alphabetical order and are used also in cases of allied or complementary subjects.

It is obvious that classification by subject matter in alphabetical order is the simplest, most flexible and least costly method, providing that definite rules are laid down for defining the subjects. Each subject should in fact be defined in writing, its content fixed, its limits and its relationship, if any, with the other topics.

Ideally the number of subjects should be limited, so as to reduce the possibilities of error, doubts and duplications to a minimum. When it is not possible to decide on all the subjects in advance, only the person responsible should add new subjects, after careful consideration. He will look over the subjects already covered in order to make sure that no synonyms or ambiguities are allowed in.

E

It is advisable to go over the whole of the classification system periodically in order to correct errors, make necessary changes and bring things up to date.

In conclusion, many of the drawbacks of classification by subject matter in alphabetical order can be eliminated or minimized if the subjects are selected, kept up to date and maintained systematically. If this is not done, the classification, because of its open character, will quickly become a mass of subjects which multiply themselves according to varying rules, do not follow their own logic and are frequently of dubious meaning.

6.4 NUMERICAL AND ALPHANUMERICAL CLASSIFICATION BY SUBJECT MATTER

It sometimes happens that classification by subject matter in alphabetical order does not represent the most satisfactory answer for certain needs. This is especially true in the case of classifications which are to be sub-divided further and when it is found useful to group together topics of a similar nature.

In such circumstances the material can be classified numerically or alphanumerically in such a way as to permit the subjects to be broken down further or, vice versa, to group them in larger categories. However, it might be as well to point out that a system using purely alphabetical symbols is rarely used.

It is hardly necessary to point out that numerical classification by subject matter involves organizing the subjects consecutively according to the number allotted to them, and not alphabetically.

According to the most popular system of numerical classification, the subjects are grouped into categories and these into even larger classes and so on, with as many groupings being created as necessary.

In practice, however, the preparatory work is done in the opposite order. First of all the large sub-divisions are established, then each one of them is divided into classes (which can be unlimited in number), and these in turn are divided into sub-classes and so on. Each division is given a number, which is separated from the class number by a point or oblique. The same applies to the division of the sub-classes: e.g.

33 Building materials
33.1 Cement
33.1.1 Portland

33.1.2 White Portland
33.1.3 Firm setting
. . . .
   33.2 Other materials
     33.2.1 Accelerators
. . . .

In place of the numerical system, the alphanumerical system can be used whereby the first division is indicated by a number, the next one by a letter and so on: e.g.

  33 Building materials
    33A Cement
      33A1   Portland
      33A2   White Portland
      33A3   Firm setting
    . . . .
    33B Other materials
      33B1   Accelerators
    . . . .

As will be seen, in the latter instance it is not necessary to have points or obliques to separate the various divisions. Should the alphanumerical system be adopted it should be borne in mind that letters cannot so easily be used as numbers, since letters are harder to remember, especially when doubled, unless some way can be found to establish some sort of relationship between the code letter and the initial of the subject codified.

If there are more than 26 subdivisions in any one category, two or more letters in tandem are used: e.g.

33abd41

As compared to classification by subject matter in alphabetical order, both numerical and alphanumerical orders have the advantage (and disadvantage) of attempting a logical, rather than casual, grouping of the subjects. Compared with the Dewey system (which we shall see in the next section) they have the advantage (and disadvantage) of being 'open'. In effect, the possibility of continuously adding new subjects limits the rationality of the system, even if it makes it more flexible and able to evolve with the changing needs of the business. Apart from the problem of deciding on the subjects, this technique also presents the problem of deciding on the groupings among the various subjects, i.e. the classification system itself. The classes and sub-classes must be clearly distinguished, have logical meaning and fill well-defined needs. In other words, abstract schemes and formal perfection are to be avoided. If this objective is realized, the technique of classification by subject matter in numerical or alphanumerical order will yield the greatest advantage, and make up for the complications which it inevitably brings with it.

The system must be flexible, that is, able to absorb new categories or classes and sub-classes as needed. This will be possible if each of the divisions decided upon has a definite content, enabling others to be added without the slightest conflict.

In conclusion, when the system is organized an attempt should not be made to establish a relationship between the various categories, but only within each category. The categories must not be enormous in content and must be clearly distinguished between each other. The internal sub-division must be clear and functional without going into superfluous details.

The need to set up an index with the subjects in alphabetical order to facilitate retrieval and the great complexity of filing and retrieval make this a more costly system than classification by subject matter in alphabetical order.

6.5   DEWEY DECIMAL CLASSIFICATION

Like the numerical and alphanumerical systems, the Dewey decimal classification technique consists of a grouping into classes of a few main subjects, divided and sub-divided various times, each main subject and its sub-divisions having a numerical or alphabetical indication to facilitate the search for the various items.

This type of classification was used for the first time by Dewey in 1870 in a library. His object was to group all human knowledge into ten main groups. From the practical point of view this aim would appear to be impossible, but Dewey succeeded and in a very rational way.

Obviously, each of the ten main categories was subsequently divided into ten sub-categories, which were in turn broken down into ten further divisions, which were again divided into ten.

Later on the decimal system, which attracted many scholars because of its formal perfection, was used in other applications, the main one in the business world being the book-keeping system.

In contrast to the alphabetical, numerical, and alphanumerical systems previously described, which are open, the Dewey decimal system is closed. While in the systems mentioned it is always possible to add sub-divisions to a given category or sub-category if it should be deemed necessary, this is not possible in the decimal system, since there can be no more than ten categories or sub-categories. This is a serious drawback, so much so that this system is only to be adopted when absolutely necessary.

If it were decided to adopt this system in a filing department, the material would have to be divided into ten main sections, each one of which would be divided in turn into ten sub-sections. In this way if 'Labour' were a main grouping, we would get:

    4 Labour
        4.0 Applications for employment
        4.1 Statistics on staff services
        4.2 Statistics on staff remuneration
        4.3 Labour disputes
        . . . .
        4.9 . . . .

The sub-sections could also be broken down in the same way. For instance:

    4 Labour
        . . . .
        4.3 Labour disputes
            4.3.0 Labour disputes amicably resolved
            4.3.1 Labour dispute laws
            . . . .
            4.3.9 . . . .
        . . . .

With the Dewey system, as with the numerical and alpha-numerical systems it is almost always necessary to have an index in alphabetical order to facilitate the search for the various headings. Dewey attempted to find a way to facilitate the search by memorizing part of the basic division between the ten main subjects and their respective numbers, as well as how these position numbers relate to each other. However, such expedients have little practical value.

With a decimal classification it is necessary to set up the whole system right away, taking into account also future subjects. Further, the system must be set up by an especially experienced person, who has a deep knowledge not only of the material being classified and its purpose, but also of probable future needs. If such is not the case, the system will quickly become obsolete, a useless superstructure of no practical value in which both filing and retrieval has become extremely hard work.

An error frequently made in setting up a decimal classification system is to establish the divisions superficially, according to abstract rules or with a view to achieving a formally perfect order. It is not easy to make a proportionate analysis of the various groups of subjects, since the large sub-divisions are seldom equal in practical importance and in content of material to be filed.

Finally, the need to leave space for possible future headings without modifying the plan can result in outlandish solutions being sought rendering the system more complex yet still not taking every eventuality into account.

These drawbacks of the decimal classification can be reduced when it is used only for division into broad categories. For instance, in the case of a correspondence file, the decimal system can be adopted to divide it into broad categories, then each category can be classified in alphabetical, geographical or chronological order.

In any event, it is advisable to avoid too detailed a classification, if only to cut down on the expense involved in more complex refinements and to reduce the risk of the plan becoming obsolete.

Because of the need to divide the subjects into broad categories, the rules governing the decimal classification vary more rapidly than with other systems. Dewey described how in his system topics relating to the heading 'Liquor' were at first classified under 'Temperance', a sub-group of the subject 'Ethics'. Later on he suggested that the heading be transferred to the group whose main topic was 'Medicine', in view of the medicinal qualities of alcohol. Finally, in a third move, because of the prohibition agitation at the time in the USA the same heading was transferred to the group 'Legal regulations'.

When setting up a classification system by subject matter it is also advisable to start off by writing down each subject on a card, then to gather all the cards together and check the brevity, clarity, exactness, and uniformity of the rules followed in selecting the various topics. Dewey observes that this index 'must contain all the details about each heading, giving all synonyms or alternative indications to facilitate as much as possible the research work by inserting these among the cross-reference cards. Although, in practice, the person consulting the index will learn which is the best way to do so, references and cross-references are always useful to track down related or complementary material, etc. It is advisable for the cross-references to be in the classification system as well as in the alphabetical index.'

6.6 CLASSIFICATION BY CATEGORY OR CLASS

In some cases classification is made by dividing the material into categories or classes relating to the physical or at any rate formal characteristics of the material. For instance, a library may classify books according to format, i.e. Demy Octavo, Crown Quarto and so on. Within each format the books can be sub-divided by author, subject matter, date of arrival, or other system. The reason for such a classification is to make rational use of the bookshelves, which can then have a standard distance between them.

Another example of division by category is the separation of material in a filing cabinet according to length of conservation, i.e. up to six months, between six months and a year, from one to three years, from three to five years, over five years. Or again arranging the customer card-index in order of importance, and so on.

Classification 'by category', when correctly done and not pushed beyond certain limits, is particularly useful, since it facilitates control, examination, comparison, etc., or it can permit space to be better utilized or special equipment to be used. It must however be borne in mind that the first requisite of classification is simplicity. Frequently, the advantages of classification by category are lost in the greater complexity of the system, with a resulting increase in the possibility of error and higher upkeep cost.

7

CLASSIFICATION IN CHRONOLOGICAL ORDER

7.1 DEFINITION

Classification in chronological order means filing the material progressively according to date of issue, manufacture, purchase, expiry, receipt, etc., generally putting the oldest date at the bottom and the more recent on top.

7.2 ADVANTAGES AND DISADVANTAGES

Classification in chronological order is one of the quickest and cheapest methods, since it can be done by staff with little training in a short time and using little space, since interpolations are not called for, but only superpositions or additions of new material. In order to find the material again, however, it is necessary to know the date under which it has been filed. It follows, therefore, that this method is suitable when:

> The material filed is of limited quantity and therefore quick to sort.
> It is possible to know, at least approximately, the date it was filed.
> There are particular aims in view.

Classification in chronological order is in addition extremely useful for filing financial documents. If, for instance, an invoice payable in 60 days becomes due on December 31, by using a chronological classification system, it will be possible to file it at the correct due date. At the appropriate time it will therefore be possible to check to see whether payment has been made or whether a reminder should be sent out, etc.

Classification in chronological order is also advisable as a subsidiary filing method. In the illustration given, for instance, it would be good practice to keep one copy of the invoice filed in alphabetical or numerical order under the customer's name and the other in the due date file. In small and medium-sized businesses this method can be used for setting up a centralized 'due date' or reminder filing system. In this way anyone needing to put a due date on a payment, or to send a reminder on a given date, or to meet a commitment on a given date, simply sends the original document or a copy to the filing clerk in charge of the 'due date' file. The clerk files all these documents daily in chronological order and as the due date arrives, he returns the document to the person who originally gave it to him. This system is quite simple and its cost is very low.

7.3 THE CLASSIFICATION CRITERIA

In order to facilitate the addition and retrieval of material, it is usually divided into groups, which in turn are divided into sections.

The groups are determined according to the quantity of material to be filed and can be made up of:

The months of the year
Fortnights
Ten days
Weeks
Days

or any other period which is considered useful.

The sections are also determined according to the amount of material in each group and can be made up of:

Ten days.
Weeks.
Days.

Within each section the material is divided:

Alphabetically.
Numerically.

Here is an example of a chronological/alphabetical classification:

1963—May
2
A—N
O—Z
3
A—N
O—Z
etc.

If the chronological/numerical system is adopted, then the material within each section can be ordered:

According to the registration number of arrival or mailing (if it is correspondence);
According to its consecutive number (receipts, delivery notes, invoices, cheques, etc.);
According to other criteria.

Very frequently chronological classification is used as a final ordering criterion for material already classified according to other criteria. For instance, a cabinet containing correspondence can be classified by name in alphabetical order and, in turn, all folders pertaining to one person or one company are put into chronological order.

Other times chronological classification is used not to facilitate retrieval of the material filed, but simply to reduce the amount of space occupied. Such can be the case in a library, where books are numbered upon arrival and placed on the shelves in that order.

In such cases an index is usually made out by author in alphabetical order or by subject matter, in order to facilitate the location of the books.

Part II

ORGANIZING THE FILES

8
HOW TO FILE

8.1 THE NEED TO ORGANIZE FILES

From what we have seen thus far it is obvious that files are gradually becoming an instrument of control—a fly-wheel almost—permitting the flow of documents to be disciplined in such a way as to render it more in tune with the real needs of a business. To achieve this result it is necessary to abandon the old and outmoded concept of looking upon files as a simple storage of documents, where the needed folder is almost always irretrievable. It is necessary, on the contrary, to look upon the filing department as a place where all documents of interest to the business are tidily collected in order to ensure their perfect preservation and to guarantee swift service to all requests for the documents coming from the various departments of the company.

In other words, this instrument must be put in a position to satisfy the following fundamental needs:

1 Preservation must be orderly: it is therefore not possible to state the preservation problem without first having solved the connected problems of classification and codification of the documents to be preserved.

2 Requests for files must be filled quickly: it would be absurd if the poor organization of the files were to prejudice the departments using them, forcing them to wait and waste precious time.

The need mentioned in (1) has been suitably developed in Part I of this volume. We shall now proceed to analyse the implications of the second point.

8.2 THE ADVISABILITY OF THINNING OUT THE FILES

We have already established that it is necessary to set up a filing system because:

All businesses are obliged, by law, to preserve for a number of years, which vary according to the particular regulations in force, all documents which are connected with the transactions entered upon by the businesses themselves. In practice, many of these documents are kept for longer periods.

Together with official documents, as mentioned above, every company produces and wishes to preserve documents which have a certain operative value and have, as it were, a semi-official character. Frequently such documents are kept for even longer periods than those mentioned above.

Finally, in order to carry out its activities, a company must preserve a number of papers of the most varied kinds.

All of this means that in order to carry out this activity, which involves a vast amount of paper-work, in the best possible way, it is necessary to defray a cost which is almost always rather high and the exact extent of which companies are seldom aware. This is actually perfectly comprehensible if one bears in mind, as we have already pointed out, that the bulk of filing expenses are connected with the filing staff, which makes costs very difficult to calculate exactly.

Independently from calculating the actual cost, it is possible, and we feel useful, to attempt to pin down the main causes which condition the cost and to find solutions leading to its reduction. In other words, we shall attempt to lay down a few general rules which companies wishing to keep filing costs to a minimum should follow.

The need to organize the files along the most convenient lines first of all raises the problem of selecting the information to be filed. In other words, the first way in which to reduce filing costs is to make a very stringent selection of the material to be preserved. The question which must be asked in each case is: Must the life of this document definitely be protracted? To answer the question it is necessary to look at it from several aspects, two of the main aspects being the value of the document and any legal or fiscal regulation involved. Another aspect which must not be overlooked is the degree of topicality which the various documents have from the point of view of the business.

It is obvious, however, that with few exceptions, one cannot decide point blank to destroy a document just because it is of no immediate use. Other reasons make it advisable, even imperative, to keep it for some considerable time. It then becomes obvious that this need results in more voluminous files to the detriment of their functionality.

8.3   DIFFERENT LEVELS OF FILING

There are only two ways out of this dead-end:

> To set very definite rules for the conservation of the documents, specifying in each case how long they should be kept and spot-checking the files to make sure that instructions have been carried out and the filing clerks have not interpreted them arbitrarily.

> Establish a life cycle for the various documents and organize the files along these lines.

There is little to add to the first point. It is sufficient to bear in mind that frequently it is more convenient to seek out a piece of information again than to preserve it indefinitely.

The second point, on the other hand, deserves to be gone into in greater depth.

The truth about files is (as we have thus far set it down and it would be absurd to presume, miraculously, to reverse) the trend for papers to flow in ever greater number. A little common sense enables many useless documents to be eliminated, but in essence the problem remains unaltered. To solve it successfully it must be tackled at the organizational level.

The files—this is the point—must be easily accessible in all their component parts. To this end, the first consideration to be borne in mind is this: the frequency with which a document is referred to varies in direct proportion to the degree of up-to-dateness of the document concerned. In other words, the more up to date a document is, the more frequently it will be referred to.

Having postulated this premise it becomes possible to outline the first broad solution to the problem, which can be synthesized as follows: A filing system, in order to carry out its functions adequately, must be organized at various levels, according to the degree of topicality of the documents it contains.

It remains to decide what these levels must be.

So far most companies have settled for a minimal solution, dividing the files into two sections:

A so-called 'Active' section, which includes all documents which are referred to fairly frequently.

A so-called 'Inactive' section, seldom referred to, in which all documents of a purely documentary value are preserved until the time is ripe for their destruction.

Such a division is not considered sufficient, however, since it confronts its organizers with the problem of whether the active files should be structurally centralized or decentralized, which clearly brings out the need to create additional levels of filing. Clearly, if the files are organized in the light of the principle whereby the documents must quickly be available each time they are needed, a form of decentralization is desirable, since it brings the documents nearer to their probable users.

The obstacles to decentralization are also of an organizational nature. It is in fact only possible to decentralize if there is a good organization, or, if you prefer, if tasks and responsibilities are clearly set out. One has only to bear in mind the fact that, if lines of responsibility are not drawn up without any shadow of a doubt, documents cannot be brought close to their users, since the latter are difficult to identify. In such a case, decentralization is further inadvisable since, if other offices needed to refer to the documents, they would not know exactly who to turn to for them.

Assuming, however, that what we have called 'a good organiz-ation' exists, decentralization appears to be a solution likely to make the filing system more functional and cheaper to run.

The guiding lines for gradually bringing the files closer to the offices using them are:

On the one hand it is necessary to eliminate the single, central-ized 'Active' file and substitute it with as many files as there are company departments, i.e. administration, production, sales, etc.

On the other hand it is necessary to separate the 'newer' documents on the basis of which very urgent action has to be taken, from those which have lost their immediate operative importance and have become a 'justification' of action already taken.

The decentralization broadly outlined by the above two points will radically transform the face of the filing. In effect the documents will be more carefully divided according to topicality.

This will give us the first section of the filing system, with the documents and papers newly arrived or needing urgent attention or follow-through being preserved in the department using them. According to the new terminology which we advocate, this, and this alone, is the 'active file'.

The second section of the filing system is at department head level and contains all the documents which have been discarded from the active files once all operations called for have been carried out. This section is called the 'Semi-active file' and its purpose is to supply the necessary data to control the operations carried out.

The third section is the traditional one and is the only one which it is advisable to centralize. It is called, as before, the 'Inactive File' and contains all papers which have all but lost their operational value and have acquired a purely documentary role.

The value of this important company service thereby becomes more functional, since it fills one of the greatest of business needs— the prompt availability of information.

The idea of making this new separation of the material to be filed has been seized on also by the manufacturers of office equipment, who are marketing desks with deep-filing drawers and small cabinets equipped with suspension files, thereby institutionalizing the 'Active File' in the meaning we have given to it.

It is hardly necessary to emphasize the fact that the organization suggested is the most rational one and the one most conducive to a more functional and economical utilization of the filing services. We shall therefore keep to this scheme in the following chapters.

9
ORGANIZING THE ACTIVE FILES

9.1 THE ADVISABILITY OF SUB-DIVIDING THE MATERIAL FILED

In order to make files more efficient, that is, to speed up retrieval and re-filing of the material, it is advisable to decentralize the location of the documents as much as possible. We have already explained why this solution is the best one.

At the same time we have also established that efficiency is in direct relationship to the topicality of the documents in the files and consequently we have demonstrated the usefulness of dividing the files into three types:

Active files.
Semi-active files.
Inactive files.

In tackling the problem of organizing the files we shall keep to this distinction.

The present chapter is devoted to organizing the active files.

9.2 THE ARRIVAL OF DOCUMENTS

The active files are mainly supplied by the incoming mail. This is usually sorted and passed on to the various departments according to the particular instructions laid down by the management.

The mail is frequently identified in an impersonal way, since letters are often addressed to an individual not by name, but by function.

In order to save time it would be advisable for the people in charge of sorting the incoming mail to do some preliminary classifying of the material. To this effect we suggest a simple, quick, and precise method which will facilitate the work for the people receiving the mail. The method consists in separating the documents relating to important or urgent matters from papers of a purely informative or documentary character. Material can be sorted into four groups:

Action.
Information.
Documentation.
Personal and confidential.

In this way the addressee can ascertain, without useless and harmful loss of time, the priorities of the work to be done, the business to be transacted and the decisions to be made.

In any event, if this work cannot be entrusted to the secretaries—and the work is simple enough if precise rules are laid down—then it must be done by the addressee, since this preliminary sorting is basic for the active file.

Within the four groups the material can then be sorted as follows:

All documents which will initiate, continue or conclude action in subject order.
All documents and forms of an informative character in chronological order.
All documents of a documentary nature in alphabetical order.
Personal and confidential matters, which are generally few in number, in subject order.

The material relating to the four groups should then be transferred, properly ordered, into folders. The addressee must then further classify the documents sent to him for action in order of urgency and file them in different folders, preferably of another colour.

These files should be limited in number by the individual company, in order to avoid an exaggerated subdivision of the material with the resulting difficulty of retrieving it.

A possible sub-division would be the following:

1 LETTERS AWAITING A REPLY FROM OUTSIDE This heading would include all documents awaiting acknowledgment from one or more correspondents.

2 REPLIES HELD UP FOR INTERNAL REASONS This heading would include all documents needing a reply requiring some research or thought on the part of the addressee.

3 REPLIES ALREADY MADE This heading would include all documents that:

 a Have already been replied to, definitely settling the problem and awaiting no further action. These documents are temporarily classified, pending their despatch to the semi-active files.

 b Have already had a reply in regard to a particular problem, but must not be definitely filed. The reply may be a useful source of information or a pretext to initiate new action either connected or unconnected with the original subject.

The contents of the files can be identified by means of an index or multicoloured markers according to a code which each company can devise for itself.

While he is classifying the documents received, the addressee can underline the items under which the documents will in due course have to be filed or, in their absence, write down the code by which the document will henceforth be known. All this must be done according to the rules laid down by the company. It should not be forgotten that the 'action—information—documentation' subdivision should be abandoned as soon as the material goes on to the semi-active file.

With regard to the identification of the various groups of documents, it is advisable to make extensive use of colour and other synoptic markings, i.e. indexes and tabs which enable the active file to be organized rationally and inexpensively at the working post.

9.3   PLANNING THE WORKING POST

In order to carry out a plan whereby the documents gradually go from the active to the semi-active files and thence to the inactive files, it is necessary first of all to have a properly organized place of work, the main seat of the active files.

The principle 'maximum volume in minimum space' is frequently ignored.

In order to attain this key-objective it is indispensable to make a preliminary analysis of each working post, within each function, before deciding on the equipment to be purchased. Chief executives must realize that administrative productivity does not consist merely in acquiring modern equipment, but first of all *in organizing the work post*, perhaps with the aid of outside specialists.

Such an analysis calls for the drawing up of a detailed organization chart of the functional structure of the various offices or departments, a diagram showing the circulation of all printed matter, forms and administrative documents, a rough analysis of the quantity and nature of the documents to be classified at the working post.

There follows an improvement:

In the selection and normalization of the material.

In the layout of the furniture and equipment within the offices.

In the elimination of useless and therefore unproductive movements.

In the grouping together of similar functions with a view to eliminating unnecessary movement and reducing transcriptions (centralized filing within each department).

9.4 SELECTION AND CHOICE OF EQUIPMENT FOR A FUNCTIONAL WORKING POST

We have already established that the active file can be subdivided into three main categories corresponding to action, information, and documentation (plus a fourth not very voluminous category, confidential documents). These categories will serve to localize classification within the filing cabinets. Obviously the respective size of each category will depend upon the nature of the work being carried out at the particular working post under review, but they are always valid, regardless of the nature of the work being carried out.

As already mentioned, the office equipment market offers a number of solutions to satisfy the particular needs of an active file. Yet it is a fact that companies can only equip themselves satisfactorily if they first of all study and then organize the sequence of administrative work, and especially classification of documents, with a view to adapting them to a harmonious, coherent, and functional whole.

In this context it seems obvious that the type of equipment best suited to the rational organization of the working post is the modular type of desk which can be arranged in extremely functional ways. Typical examples are the L and U shaped desks.

This means that preference should be given to office furniture, and particularly desks, of the sectional type, or if preferred those which can be complemented with additional accessories, i.e. extra work surfaces, auxiliary drawers, etc. which fulfil the purpose of concentrating the maximum amount of material in a minimum amount of space and answering the needs of each employee to perfection. Such furniture is always fitted with deep filing drawers or other facilities for storing suspended files or other types of folders.

In any event the point to bear in mind is that the employees work in a sitting position. Consequently the office furniture should only be chosen after a careful study has been made of the work they do and the furniture selected should enable most of the work to be carried out from a sitting position. The choice should be further conditioned by the type of documents to be classified and how frequently they will need to be referred to.

In the case of work which is carried out in sequence, collective working posts should be provided, with connecting working surfaces and all the accessories which enable the various operations to be carried out smoothly, without any need for the employees to move about a great deal. Collective working posts also permit the joint use of some office machines, such as typewriters and calculating machines.

In the unlikely event that the modular office furniture chosen has insufficient filing capacity, one or more additional filing cabinets equipped with suspension files can be acquired. These cabinets should have no more than two shelves and must be located in the immediate vicinity of the working post (3–4 ft) so as to conserve movement, time, and energy. If they are located at the distance indicated it is not even necessary to get up from one's chair in order to reach them.

Auxiliary equipment which is not a part of the modular furniture includes suspension file cupboards, which can take care of exceptionally large active filing requirements.

In any event, one thing is certain: the suspended file, whether affording lateral or vertical vision, is the most important element of modern rational classification, because it is the most accessible.

It is not advisable to use filing cabinets with drawers or cupboards without sliding doors for active filing because they take up too much space and consequently require frequent movements for filing and retrieving the material.

If we have emphasised the functionality of suspended files and modular office furniture, this does not mean that the problem of active filing cannot be solved in other ways, especially by using traditional types of equipment. But it must be made quite clear that solutions of this nature militate against rational working methods.

Companies which want to give their employees 'made to measure working posts', based on motion study and a study of the work which each one does, must not fail to consider the notes thus far outlined.

10
ORGANIZING THE SEMI-ACTIVE FILES

10.1 ROLE OF THE OFFICER IN CHARGE OF THE SEMI-ACTIVE FILES

In the process of decentralization outlined in the first chapter of this Part of the book, the semi-active files have been assigned the role of files at the operational department level (administration, sales, etc.). Consequently, each company can have as many semi-active files as there are departments.

The general responsibility for the management of each of these filing units will be given to the head of the department to which they are attached, while the day-to-day responsibility for them will be given to a person which we shall identify right away by the name of 'officer in charge of the semi-active files'. To this officer will be delegated the strict adherence to the filing rules in his department.

The choice of these officers can be made from among the senior employees, who are well acquainted with the administrative workings of their department. The main purpose of this choice is to restate the function of the files which has usually not been given the importance it deserves.

The main tasks entrusted to the officer in charge of the semi-active files are:

Care of the perfect preservation of the documents.
Continuous up-dating of the files.
Retrieval of the files as requested and carrying out of all formalities required of him.
Thinning out of the files, as documents which have lost their topicality are sent to the inactive filing department.
Control and co-ordination of traffic with the inactive files and any requests connected with it.

The bulk of these activities can involve a volume of work which will vary from company to company and, within the same company, from department to department. Apart from very exceptional cases, the volume of work will never justify a person being employed full time on it, even if his or her presence is continuously required in order to satisfy requests for files without delay.

It follows that one of the advantages of decentralizing the filing system—and by no means a secondary advantage—is that it eliminates one of the main drawbacks of centralized systems, i.e. the delay in carrying out the work.

At the same time, the bulk of these activities affords each company department order and safety as far as their filing operations are concerned.

10.2 HOW TO ORGANIZE THE SEMI-ACTIVE FILES

Having established the guiding principle that decentralization is the way to organize the filing, it immediately becomes obvious that there are at least two ways of correctly running the semi-active files:

> The filing equipment can be placed in the same premises as the working posts.
>
> The equipment can be placed in adjacent premises or otherwise close to the working posts.

The choice of one or the other solution, as well as the acceptability of both, will depend upon the kind of premises used and type of equipment available. The choice will also be influenced by the frequency with which the files will be used.

In order to solve the problem of the most efficient organization of the semi-active files, it is therefore necessary to carry out a little research. In particular it is necessary to:

> Draw up an outline showing the number of employees in each office, a job analysis for each one and a layout of the working posts.
>
> Study the possibilities which the existing equipment offers and that offered by new equipment on the market, in case it becomes advisable to remodernize the offices.

Determine the relative position of each group of documents within the available space and ascertain whether it is the most conducive to the proper working of the filing system.

Identify the main sectors where documents are most frequently referred to and where the most delicate searches are carried out.

If this research is properly carried out, it results in:

Better use of the available space.
Better use of the filing services, retrieval of documents being facilitated, thanks to the rational arrangement of the equipment and the documents.
Good preservation of the material and better order.
Better working of the filing system in general.

These results depend on the availability of suitable equipment, which above all must be strong and easily accessible to a filing clerk usually working from a standing position.

A recent Max Planck Institute report established that work done in a standing position requires three times as much energy as that done sitting down. Nine times as much energy is expended if the operator has to bend down and twenty times as much if he has to use a ladder or other means to reach upwards. It is therefore obvious that, for semi-active files which are referred to fairly frequently, it is not advisable to use equipment reaching up to the ceiling or which forces the filing clerk to carry out tiring climbs in order to reach the files.

In any event, only after the items listed have been evaluated should a decision be made as to whether the filing equipment should:

Be located in the same offices as the working posts.
Or be located in an adjacent or nearby office.

This, in substance, was the problem posed at the beginning of this chapter.

10.3 EQUIPMENT AVAILABLE

It is now worthwhile mentioning briefly the equipment available for a semi-active file. Without going into details on the various types of office furniture normally available on the market, which will be done in a later chapter, we are anxious to lay down the principle that the suspension filing systems are ideal for the complex and delicate problems which can occur from time to time at the semi-active level. The choice, which is mainly dictated by functional motives, is also conditioned by the fact that a similar solution has already been suggested for the active files. In practice, if the two files are standardized the double advantage is gained that the original headings can be retained and the material can be transferred without further manipulation, with consequent savings both in filing and retrieval time.

Obviously only documents can be preserved in suspended files. All the rest—books, magazines, booklets, leaflets, folders, etc., because of their disparate size and format, are best kept on horizontal shelves, using rigid separators or boxes for flimsy items which cannot stand up on their own.

While standing by the principle that easy accessibility of the material is best attained by using suspended filing equipment, we can ask ourselves whether the material should be secured to the folders by means of metal clasps. Table 10.1 establishes without the shadow of a doubt that this method is slower and consequently more expensive.

Table 10.1 COMPARISON OF TIMES NEEDED TO FILE 100 DOCUMENTS

Description of operations	File with clasps	File without clasps
1. Perforating the documents (3 to 5 documents at a time, including classification)	11 min	—
2. Preliminary sorting	22 min	22 min
3. Opening drawers of cabinets and retrieving files	12 min	12 min
4. Carrying the folders with clasps from the cabinet to the desk	8 min	—
5. Opening the clasps (which consists in loosening the laces or folding back the metal clasps)	10 min	—
6. Putting the documents in the folder. Partial internal classification in chronological, alphabetical, or numerical order, etc.	3 min	1 min
7. Securing the clasp	6 min	—
8. Putting the files back in the cabinet and closing the cabinet	9 min	1 min
TOTAL	1 h 21 min	36 min

There are, however, some documents which should by preference be attached to the folder containing them. Such documents are:

Confidential papers.

Papers which are concerned with personnel matters.

Manuscripts or important documents concerning the activities of the top management team.

Official documents relating to fiscal, insurance, and other matters.

10.4 CHOOSING THE EQUIPMENT

We have examined the factors which influence the organization of the semi-active files and condition the choice of equipment. From the brief list given it is obvious that such factors must be objectively evaluated and pondered before any decision resulting in the purchase of filing equipment is made. In any event the choice should be veered towards 'polyvalent' equipment, which strikes a compromise between the conflicting needs of cutting down the floorspace covered and making the maximum use of the wall space, compatibly with the need to give easy access to the files to someone in a standing position.

Filing cupboards with suspended files are therefore the ideal way of achieving the objective with a minimum of obstruction. Filing cabinets with drawers also offer a valid solution, providing there is not a space problem, since drawers, when open, occupy twice as much space as cupboards. It is worthwhile pointing out that a filing cabinet with five drawers, taking up the same amount of space as other types of filing equipment, permits a considerably larger amount of material to be stored.

A piece of equipment which has many advantages, both in the case of the active and the semi-active files, is the drum file in which the suspended files are mounted on a support which rotates around a central axis.

10.5 HOW TO FILE MATERIAL IN THE SEMI-ACTIVE FILES

Apart from the problem of selecting the right equipment, the semi-active files also present the problem of determining the criteria by which the material to be preserved is to be filed. The solution should obviously not be left to the individual managers, but the problem should be studied as a whole, in harmony with the needs of the business. The semi-active files have features completely different from those of the active files: the first is conceived above all as a company service, whereas the second is mainly conceived to facilitate the work of the individual offices. It is therefore above all in the first case that the need arises for an organic classification system, which permits everyone to get at the filed material without difficulty.

In order to give the system real value, which does not permit anyone to change it on his own initiative, it is further necessary that it be ratified by written rules, approved by top management, who would recognize it as having the same value as any other company procedure. Even modifications to the rules should be submitted to top management for approval before they become operative.

Only in this way can the files become a management tool which serves as a stimulus rather than a hindrance to the whole company organization.

Having made this premise, we feel it necessary to point out once again that in order to reach the objective of transforming the files into a management tool it is necessary to leave them a certain amount of flexibility, avoiding excessive bureaucratization.

This can be achieved if complete decentralization is avoided, limiting it, at most, to department level (sales, administration, production, etc.).

It is in this context that we shall attempt to see how a classification system can be devised. Ours will obviously only be general rules, since each company must adapt the system to its own specific needs.

10.6 THE FILES OF THE SALES DIVISION

10.6.1 CONTENT

The files of a sales division will normally contain documents of the following type:

> Customer correspondence (incoming and outgoing).
> Correspondence with salesmen and with branches or outlying offices (including reports on the work carried out by each operating unit).
> Copies of orders and order confirmations.
> Rules, instructions, and internal circulars.

Market reports and reports on the competition.
Catalogues, folders, etc.
Confidential information.

10.6.2 CUSTOMER CORRESPONDENCE
We shall now attempt to determine the most suitable criteria for classifying the documents listed.

Customer correspondence can be classified as follows, depending on the particular company situation:

In alphabetical–chronological order.
In geographical–alphabetical–chronological order.

The first method is particularly suitable for companies which do not have a very large number of customers and therefore do not feel the need to divide them into areas. In such cases filing in alphabetical–chronological order is the simplest solution. Each customer of any importance is given a separate file and the files are then put into alphabetical order. Small customers can be filed under 'Miscellaneous'. Within each folder the letters are filed in chronological order.

Geographical–alphabetical–chronological order, on the other hand, is recommended for companies with a large number of customers. In this case the problem is to decide to what extent the material should be divided geographically. Some companies divide their markets into sales areas, while others stick to geographical divisions (into counties, towns, etc.). For some companies it is sufficient to stop at the first sub-division; others find it necessary to divide the material according to their salesmen's routes; others again need to go even further and divide the material into street and number (public utility organizations come under this heading). As can be seen, there are a number of solutions from which a company can choose the one which fills its own needs best, having first made a careful study of what these needs are.

As for the filing rules, the following indications are valid: within the last geographical sub-division the material is filed alphabetically, while the documents relative to each name are put into chronological order.

10.6.3 CORRESPONDENCE WITH SALESMEN
Correspondence with salesmen, branches or distant offices, as

well as salesmen's reports should be filed in alphabetical order according to salesman or branch. Since in some cases each individual file can become quite voluminous, it is advisable further to divide the material according to subject matter, within the file.

10.6.4 ORDER CONFIRMATIONS
It is advisable to file order confirmations or copies of orders together with the rest of the material in each customer's file (correspondence, etc.). There are therefore no particular filing problems. At the outside, one might put all order confirmations together, separating them from the correspondence, thereby making a separation by subject matter.

10.6.5 RULES, INSTRUCTIONS, AND CIRCULARS
Rules, instructions and circulars are best classified by subject matter and within each topic, in chronological order.

10.6.6 MARKET DOCUMENTATION AND INFORMATION ON THE COMPETITION
Market documentation and information on the competition should be classified in geographical order, keeping as far as possible to the division brought about by the correspondence. Obviously, each geographical division should contain both the market documentation and the information on the competition, appropriately divided.

The latter, however, should be further divided according to product or under the various competitors' names. Since most of the information on the competition consists of catalogues or folders, it is best, in the interests of a flexible filing system, to throw out an old catalogue as soon as a new one arrives, having first made sure that the new material does indeed supersede the old.

10.6.7 CATALOGUES, FOLDERS, ETC.
The catalogues, folders, etc. which every company produces to document its customers on its products must be filed according to the product or group of products to which they refer.

10.6.8 CONFIDENTIAL MATERIAL
Confidential material, whichever office it may belong to, is usually filed by subject matter. It should be kept in the office of the executive concerned so that no one else has access to it.

10.6.9 OTHER MATERIAL

Any other material should be filed according to criteria which are considered suitable as the occasion arises. In the case of companies with a large sales organization divided into several branches, it is advisable for each branch to keep files of the material which concerns it. In such cases it becomes necessary to have duplicates of original documents. Apart from material of purely local interest, branches should therefore keep copies of incoming and outgoing correspondence, as well as copies of orders agreed upon with customers. The originals should be sent to head office.

10.7 THE FILES OF THE ADMINISTRATIVE DIVISION

10.7.1 CONTENTS

The files of the administrative division contain, for the purposes of the present work, all the material relative to the purchasing and personnel offices, which, particularly in the case of large companies, it is often advisable to keep separate. The main categories of documents included in this section are:

Invoices.
Book-keeping documents.
Tax matters of all kinds.
Correspondence.
Contracts.
Purchasing office documents.
Personnel documents.
Rules and instructions.
Minutes of Board of directors meetings.
Confidential documents.

10.7.2 INVOICES

It is necessary to distinguish between sales invoices and purchase invoices.

Sales invoices must, by law, be made out in duplicate. The top copy is normally classified in progressive numerical order, in accordance with the prevailing regulations. The second copy can be classified in such a way as to permit a check on whether the transaction has come to a satisfactory conclusion (usually in chronological order according to due date). Such a classification is, by its very nature, temporary. Once the transaction is concluded, this copy of the invoice can go to complete the documentation of the customer concerned, in the corresponding file (which is kept, as we have seen, in the sales division).

Purchase invoices must also be numbered. They can be filed definitely in one of two ways:

In numerical order.

In alphabetical order under the name of the suppliers.

The first method is not to be recommended, since it is difficult to find an invoice unless its number is known. The second method is definitely to be recommended. However, before incoming invoices are definitely filed, they must be dealt with from the administrative point of view. In the meantime, therefore, they can be filed in chronological order by due date.

10.7.3   BOOK-KEEPING DOCUMENTS

Book-keeping documents are best classified according to subject matter (receipts, balance sheets, invoice books, etc.) and within each topic in chronological or numerical order according to individual needs or legal requirements. In the case of companies with a properly codified accounting system, documents pertaining to the various accounts should be classified by using the same symbols which distinguish the accounts themselves.

10.7.4   FISCAL MATTERS

Documents pertaining to taxes falling due on certain dates should be kept in the active files of the Chief Accountant or Company Secretary. Once payment has been made, the documents in question must be transferred to the semi-active files and classified by type of tax. They should be conserved there together with any other material pertaining to each tax paid.

10.7.5   CORRESPONDENCE

Correspondence or any type of written communication with customers (extracts of accounts, etc.) should be filed in the customer file in the sales division.

10.7.6   CONTRACTS

Contracts directly concerned with company assets (purchases and sales, rent, etc.) can simply be classified in chronological order, if they are not numerous, or by subject matter.

10.7.7 PURCHASING OFFICE DOCUMENTS

Documentation relating to the purchasing office can be divided into two main categories:

Material relating to communications with suppliers.
Material regarding possible sources of supply.

Material relating to communications with suppliers is best classified in alphabetical order by supplier.

Material regarding possible sources of supply, on the other hand, is best filed according to type of product.

10.7.8 PERSONNEL OFFICE DOCUMENTS

The documents preserved by a personnel office are usually extremely varied and complex. The main category of documents to be filed are usually the following:

Documents relative to the personnel on the company payroll.
Applications for employment.

The first group of documents should be classified in alphabetical order in at least three groups: executives, employees, and manual workers.

Applications for employment, on the other hand, are best classified according to type of service offered.

10.7.9 RULES AND INSTRUCTIONS

Rules and instructions are best classified according to subject matter and, thereafter, in chronological order.

10.7.10 MINUTES OF BOARD MEETINGS, ETC.

Minutes of Board meetings and similar documents should be kept in suitable binders and given an analytical index, divided by subject matter.

10.7.11 CONFIDENTIAL MATERIAL

Confidential material, to whichever office it may belong, is usually filed according to subject matter and kept in the office of the executive to whom it belongs.

G

10.8 THE FILES OF THE PRODUCTION DIVISION

10.8.1 CONTENT

The semi-active files of the production division mainly contain documents of the following type:

Documents connected with the plant and equipment.
Documents connected with work cycles.
Patents.

It is necessary to point out that the classification rules vary according to how the company is organized.

10.8.2 DOCUMENTS CONNECTED WITH THE PLANT AND EQUIPMENT

Documents concerning the equipment can either be classified according to the type of equipment or by department or work-shop, and, within this heading according to type of equipment.

10.8.3 DOCUMENTS CONNECTED WITH WORK CYCLES

Documents relative to work cycles, which can consist of time-study sheets, technical drawings, etc. can either be classified by department or work-shop, or by the number of job it refers to.

10.8.4 PATENTS

It is a well-known fact that patents are numbered consecutively. For a rational conservation of such material one can therefore either follow the official numerical order or a special numerical order established by the file. Obviously, it is necessary to have the necessary card-index for the cross-references to the inventor's name, the name of the company having the exclusive rights to the patent and the type of product invented.

11
ORGANIZING THE INACTIVE FILES

11.1 THE IMPORTANCE OF A RATIONAL ORGANIZATION OF THE INACTIVE FILES

The inactive files are the last link in the chain constituted by the various possible levels of document preservation. Consequently it must supply proof of the efficiency of the whole system. Usually insufficient importance is given to the inactive files, since it is felt that they have acquired purely historical interest, are devoid of any operational value and are only being stored until the moment for their destruction arrives.

While this is partly true, it should not be forgotten that even inactive files are occasionally called for. It should always be remembered that the efficiency of the active and semi-active files depends on the existence of the inactive files.

In effect, the inactive files are replenished by:

The active files, which passes on those documents (very few, it is true) which it is not considered necessary to transfer to the semi-active files.

The semi-active files, which passes on the majority of its material, according to the rules in force in each company.

11.2 GENERAL REMARKS ON ORGANIZING THE INACTIVE FILES

Having made this premise, it is necessary to see which documents add up to form the inactive files. Their selection is first of all a question of common sense, although certain rules, which it is essential to lay down, must be followed.

The task of making this selection, which is a delicate and also a complex one, must be entrusted to the same people responsible for the management of the departmental semi-active files, to whom we referred in the preceding chapter. The selection consists in separating the useful documents from those which are not, with the object of permitting the semi-active files to maintain the maximum agility. The advantages of such a choice can be synthesized as follows:

Space is made available in the various classifications.

The time required to refer to the documents is reduced.

The use of equipment is limited and reduced in number.

If, however, the choice is not made according to precise rules and is left to the arbitrary decision of the person in charge, the consequences can be:

An increase in the material kept in the semi-active files, for fear of passing on something of importance.

The decentralization of documents which should still remain in the semi-active files, which will be detrimental to the proper functioning of the business.

Such behaviour can, at most, be convenient for the filing clerk, who should not then ask himself the usual questions: 'Who? What? Where? When? Why? How?' but should act solely on the basis of his experience.

Such a method, however, is harmful for the company which will find itself having to sustain higher costs for an inefficient filing system. Before defining the criteria which should determine the selection of documents to be passed on to the inactive files, it is therefore necessary to:

Designate and train someone to be responsible for each of the departmental files, so that the rules laid down are followed by all.

Establish 'Filing Regulations' so that the sending of documents from the semi-active files to the inactive files is regularized, together with the preservation of documents in the latter.

Look for the most suitable equipment for each category of document.

11.3 RULES FOR SENDING DOCUMENTS TO THE INACTIVE FILES

The working out of 'Filing Regulations' to be used both by the person in charge of the filing and the various users, involves the preparation of:

A list of documents to be preserved in the files with an indication of how long each of them is to be kept.

A series of rules to be followed in making up the folders and bringing the documents up to date.

A series of rules for the classification, reference, and withdrawal of the documents.

A file organized in this way works as follows:

On the dates prearranged the clerk in charge of the semi-active files removes from the folders the documents and papers which are obsolete and are of no further immediate use. The resulting saving in space enables the more important material to be preserved longer. This cuts down on staff traffic and increases productivity.

The material is sent to the inactive files in such a way as to avoid obstructions, spreading out the work according to the time available. Transfers are made by each of the semi-active files in turn, in accordance with a time-table laid down in advance, which should take into account summer close-down periods, inventory times and any other period bringing with it tasks which have absolute priority.

In order to be able to extract documents of purely historical interest from the files at speed, it is best to identify them first of all with markers, tags or other suitable conventional method.

These rules enable the filing clerk to follow the semi-active files on a day to day basis, using his judgement while the facts are still fresh in his mind. Such a procedure obviates the need of going through the whole file each time it is thinned out and making sometimes complicated assessments on each paper.

In going through the files, it is however advisable to follow these rules:

Obsolete papers, devoid of legal value, should be destroyed as soon as they are removed from the folders.

The folders thinned out as suggested above should be sent to the inactive files.

If the whole content of the folder has lost its value and at the same time its life span as fixed in the classification system has expired, it can be destroyed in its entirety without going through the inactive file.

Apart from destroying obsolete documents and transferring folders from the semi-active file to the inactive, the filing clerk must take charge of putting confidential documents (stock certificates, patents, etc.) in a safe place (strong room or safe).

The rules briefly outlined in the above four points must be worked out in more detail by each individual company, which must adapt them to its own particular needs.

As for the classification rules to be adopted for the inactive files, it is advisable to keep to the same system used in the semi-active files.

11.4 CHOICE OF EQUIPMENT FOR THE INACTIVE FILES

The choice of equipment for the inactive files is not of very great importance since, generally speaking, the choice must be guided towards low-price equipment. In this case there are no space problems, since the inactive files are almost always located in out-lying buildings, for which the rent paid is not large. Neither is there a problem of height; material can be stored in places which are accessible only by means of a ladder, since it will be needed only infrequently.

However, the choice of equipment will be conditioned by the nature of the material to be filed. Documents can take a number of different forms:

Folders.
Books, magazines, newspapers, etc.
Magnetic tapes.
Microfilms.
Drawings.
Blocks, etc.

Such a collection of material to be preserved demands the selection of different kinds of equipment to store it in, even if it is of a uniform design.

Of course, it must not be forgotten, that even for inactive files the choice of equipment must be conditioned by the frequency with which the material will be referred to and this will vary in accordance with the type of document. It would not be out of place to consider storing some folders, for which frequent call is expected, in suspended files. In all other cases a vertical system is recommended or a horizontal one, on shelves. Obviously, in the case of vertical filing, it will be necessary to insert the material into rigid supports so that it may be preserved without deterioration. Cardboard boxes (preferably the inexpensive type) are therefore very widely used in inactive files and so is equipment for binding the various documents into books (complete with cardboard cover), according to suitable rules.

11.5 RULES FOR THE PRESERVATION OF DOCUMENTS IN THE FILE

Once the selection, classification and grouping of the documents in containers has been made, each company is faced with two possibilities with regard to the rules for the preservation of the documents:

They can be preserved as they stand without any attempt to reduce them in volume.

They can be preserved in reduced dimension, volume and weight by microfilming them or putting them on tape. The originals can be destroyed, or, if reduction takes place at the semi-active file level, they can be sent to the inactive file. This last solution is to be advised when there is a shortage of space at the company's main office. If the microfilm solution is chosen, then it will be necessary to:

a Review all semi-active documents before passing on to the operative phase;
b Mark the documents or abstracts to be reproduced;
c Give exact instructions to everyone who will be concerned with having microfilms made, in order to regulate the flow of documents.

We must point out, however, that microfilming may not prove convenient, especially if the labour factor is not taken into careful consideration.

A company wishing to pare down its filing system and save space, should make a very careful study on the advisability of microfilming certain documents, since it could become quite onerous from the point of view of referring to the documents microfilmed. It is therefore necessary to analyse the problem from the point of view of the company's needs.

A separate mention must be made of the use of photostatic reproduction as a means of avoiding the removal of a document from the file. In this case it is also necessary to examine with care whether such a procedure is warranted. It is, however, more likely to be feasible, providing the people needing to consult the documents are satisfied with a photocopy. This method does have the advantage of diminishing the risk of losing the originals.

11.6   THE PURPOSES OF AN INACTIVE FILE

As we have already said, the files should not be considered purely as 'paper storage' imposed upon the company by the prevailing laws or by custom, but as an active service which aims to contribute to greater productivity. In this spirit, the organization of a dynamic filing system assumes considerable importance.

The inactive files must consequently aim at providing each company department with the following services:

Instant production of the documents requested.
Prompt despatch of requested documentation.
Orderly conservation of the documents filed, which should be kept in perfect condition.
Prompt destruction of obsolete documents.

In order to reach these objectives it is necessary to be properly organized. In particular it is essential to make it clear that material from the semi-active files should be sent to the inactive files properly arranged in appropriate containers (cardboard boxes). Once the material is received its content must be entered in two books: the arrival book and the instructions book.

The arrival book should contain the exact location in the room of the material received, as well as the nature of the material and its arrival number. This book is an indispensable tool for the filing clerk, enabling him to retrieve the material basing his search on the arrival number.

The instructions book will give a list of material to be destroyed at a given date. Each page will detail the items to be destroyed in a particular month, the items being identified by their arrival number.

11.7 REQUESTS FOR REFERENCE

Every request for a document must of necessity be made in writing. It has been proved that telephone requests frequently give rise to misunderstandings and resulting delays.

It follows that anyone wanting to consult a document or a file must fill out a form in triplicate and forward it to the inactive filing room via the person responsible for the semi-active files in his department. If the document is not easily found within its container, it is advisable to send along the whole container.

12

HOW TO ORGANIZE THE FILING OPERATION

12.1 ESTABLISHING A REGULAR FLOW OF WORK

If the aim is to improve the workings of the filing system, our first preoccupation must be to establish a regular flow of work.

It is by no means infrequent for those responsible for the active files to keep documents longer than necessary. This can be due either to a real need of the documents in the various offices or to faulty organization.

In the first case it is up to the departments concerned to find a way of speeding up their procedures. In the second instance it is up to the person in charge of the semi-active files to make sure that every office regularly sends along material at the intervals laid down. If this is not done, the defectors should be prodded.

We have already said that, as a general rule, the active files should send to the semi-active files material which has lost its immediate interest every week. In order to avoid all the files arriving at the same time, it is advisable to arrange for them to be sent on different days, especially in cases where several offices share the same semi-active files. In this way the work is distributed equitably and bottlenecks are avoided.

It is only possible to check the length of time a document has been in the active file, if a note has been made of its date of arrival.

This can be done by stamping each document with a stamp as shown in Fig. 12.1, which can also be used as a circulation slip indicating who is to peruse the document before it is sent to the files by the last person on the list.

In some cases, in order to make sure that no document is lost or does not reach the files, every item arriving by mail can be date-

Red & White Company Limited		
Addressee		Seen
1		. . . .
2		. . . .
3		. . . .
4		. . . .
Filing date		Location
. . . . .		. . . .
	Date of arrival	
	Number	

Fig. 12.1 Facsimile of a rubber stamp indicating the 'route' that a given document must take from date of arrival to filing

stamped on arrival and likewise for outgoing post, but this is a very costly procedure and is not advisable except in exceptional cases.

12.2 PREPARING THE MATERIAL

As soon as the documents have reached the semi-active files it is as well to date-stamp them in order to eliminate any possible controversy as to the date they were handed over.

Together with the date it is advisable to give each document a consecutive number to enable a check to be made on the amount of work done and to determine the slack and busy periods.

The second operation to be carried out is to divide the material into the broad categories the filing system contains. In this way, for instance, all orders, book-keeping documents and correspondence will be separated out.

The next stage will be to sub-divide the various groups of documents into the various headings under which they have to be filed. This operation requires a perfectly organized working area and sensible equipment which enables the work to be done as quickly as possible and with the minimum of fatigue.

The main rule to follow is to have a table or desk completely clear of any extraneous material. A fixed place will then have to be assigned to each group of documents in such a way that it is easily remembered by the filing clerk. Places have to be assigned according to a plan, such as, for instance:

$$
\begin{array}{cccc}
& 3 & 6 & 9 \\
& 2 & 5 & 8 \\
0 & 1 & 4 & 7
\end{array}
$$

or the arrangement shown in Fig. 12.2, which is unquestionably more rational, can be used.

Naturally, when operating in a restricted space and when there are few sub-divisions, each paper will have to be handled several times before the work is finished. In spite of this, this procedure is the quickest and the least tiring.

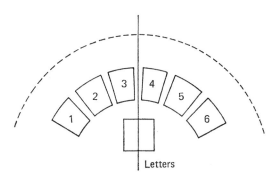

Letters

Fig. 12. 2 Arrangement of documents for sorting

For instance, if a hundred or so papers have to be sorted alphabetically, it is far more convenient to limit the first sub-division to four main groups: A–F, G–L, M–R, and S–Z and then to proceed to a further sorting into each letter of the alphabet. Generally speaking, it is not advisable to attempt to sort material into more than seven, or at most ten, groups at a time.

In order to work rapidly, good coordination is necessary. While the filing clerk is putting one document in the appropriate place, he must be reading the next one at the same time.

The sorting can also be facilitated by using special equipment. The most common type of equipment is the letter basket, of which various models are on the market. The only limitation to their use is the fact that they take up a great deal of space and if more than five

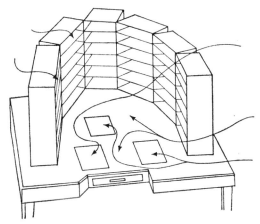

Fig. 12.3 Pigeonholes laid out on a working surface in such a way as to facilitate movements as much as possible

or six of them were used, they would take up more space than is normally available. If the baskets can be placed in rows, one on top of the other, then the limitation they present is not so great.

If the sorting job is quite a large one, it may be advisable to use the type of pigeonholes shown in Fig. 12.3, which are an improvement on the system previously mentioned. In such cases it is good practice to mark each pigeonhole with the appropriate heading.

Obviously such headings should be clearly legible so that, if a new filing clerk takes over, she will not be in difficulties.

12.3 CHOOSING THE FILING EQUIPMENT

In choosing the filing equipment the first factor to be borne in mind is the amount of filing to be done, in order to avoid the purchase of excessively costly furniture. Care should also be taken that the equipment selected ensures economy of movement on the part of the filing clerk. The fundamental rules to be observed in this connection can be summarized as follows:

The more restricted the space in which the filing is done, the less wasted movements and occasions for making errors there will be. The normal work area should be that in which the clerk can work without making physical efforts and, in any event, the work should be done in a sitting position. In other words, the need for the clerk to extend her arms excessively or take an uncomfortable position should be reduced to a minimum.

The filing clerk should be accustomed and encouraged to make use of both arms. Where possible, the hands should initiate and complete each single movement at the same time and the movements should be simple and continuous. Brusque movements should be avoided by using a suitable work area and training the staff.

The work should be organized in such a way as to require only very simple movements. The filing clerks should be accustomed to organize the work always in the same way, so that every sorting operation of a particular type is always carried out in the same way. This reduces the possibilities of error and results in quicker and more efficient filing.

As a general rule, if both arms are moved simultaneously, each one should move in the opposite direction, as this will make it easier for the clerk to keep his balance—an important factor in the reduction of fatigue. Arm movements, on the other hand, should as far as possible be symmetrical.

All documents and the necessary equipment should always be in the normal work area. A supply of pins, paper clips, ribbons, envelopes, and such like items should always be in the most convenient spot. All the material should be orderly and placed so that it can be used in a rational series of movements, which should be capable of becoming semi-automatic.

12.4 PRELIMINARY WORK

We have already said that the person in charge of the semi-active files is entrusted not only with executive tasks, but also with control. Before sorting the documents, he should therefore:

Make sure that all the documents he has received are to be conserved in the files in his charge.

Make sure that the classification details given are correct. To give but a single example, it can happen that a letterheading is not to be blindly relied upon. If, for instance, a salesman writes to his company on the letterheading of a hotel he is staying at during a selling trip, his letter will none the less have to be filed under his own name.

Make sure that all enclosures are attached to the documents, unless it is necessary to file the attachments separately.

Sort out all unimportant material from the preservation point of view (courtesy letters, sales offers, acknowledgements, etc.) in order to put it in a special 'Miscellaneous' file to be destroyed in the near future.

Mark out the most important part of each document, so that its content can be rapidly established, in case of need. For instance, a file may contain many letters from the same sender. If there is a need to find a letter about a particular subject, it is far easier to do so if the subject matter has been marked in some manner beforehand.

Make sure that the document has been seen by all the pertinent offices and departments before it is filed.

Some of the minor operations which the filing clerk should take care of before sorting the material are the following:

Mend all torn papers with transparent adhesive tape.
Fold any papers which are too large to go into the folders.

12.5   FILING THE DOCUMENTS

The checked and classified material must next be filed in the cabinets or other equipment. The method recommended for this operation is to carry the material to the cabinets to avoid taking the individual files too far from where they belong. In addition, it is advisable to take out the whole file when adding material to it, so as to avoid putting papers in the wrong place, getting two or more papers ravelled up together and so on. It is good practice never to seize a file by its tab, but to take it with both hands, holding it in on either side.

Files should never be overful and should always be easy to handle.

Two to four inches of free space should be left in all filing cabinets in order to make it easier to put in and extract files. This, however, is not necessary with cabinets which have forward-sliding fronts, enabling the whole of the space to be used.

In the case of the 'Miscellaneous' file, it is necessary periodically to extract from it any papers belonging under the same heading and opening a separate file for them. This will help to keep the 'Miscellaneous' file suitably slender.

If, as frequently happens, the filing clerk is unable to finish his day's work, he should leave all the papers received in the sorting equipment in the order they were sent to him.

In order to permit a filing clerk to catch up with a backlog of work, some companies do not give access to the filing room until a given time later in the morning, or until the previous day's filing has been done. This practice is not to be recommended, however, in view of the principle which states that the files are there to serve the company, not vice versa.

12.6   INDEXES AND CROSS-REFERENCES

In the course of describing the various classification rules we have referred to the need to keep indexes and make use of cross-references in order to facilitate consultation of the material filed. We can now go on to say that both are essential instruments, especially in certain cases.

The necessity of keeping an index is felt especially where the type of classification selected is numerical or by subject matter. In such cases it is practically impossible to identify the individual files unless they are listed alphabetically, together with their number or other identification symbol. Neither is a listing exhaustive if it does not include any necessary cross-reference from one heading to another, in order to eliminate any possible doubt.

To synthesize these two concepts into two definitions, we can say that an index is a list, in alphabetical order, made up in the same way as the headings on the individual files, which gathers together all the headings in a given classification, and is used to facilitate retrieval when the material is ordered according to other rules.

On the other hand, a cross-reference is a complement to the index, calling attention to more appropriate headings, especially in the case of synonyms or similar headings.

The important thing is for every heading to appear in the index, inasmuch as its value is measured by its completeness and the speed with which even the most unskilled researcher can find what he needs.

In addition, every index should be set up according to the following rules: it must first of all be standardized as far as the addition of new headings is concerned; it should be capable of future expansion and, finally, it should be comprehensible to everyone, not only the filing staff.

An index can be made up in a loose-leaf binder, which makes it easier to insert fresh pages, or, as is more usual, cards.

The basic unit of an index is the 'Key Word' which refers to one of the subjects in the files.

In conclusion, it should be noted that the use of an index is necessary when:

A numerical classification system is adopted, since it is only possible to identify a subject filed under a given number, if all the subjects are listed alphabetically.

Material is classified by subject matter, since which material is filed under which subject matter is more easily deduced from an index. In such cases the most commonly used procedure is to include in the index every main subject, each of its sub-divisions and every cross-index.

It is desired to identify more easily coded headings.

As for cross-references, there is no need for them to have a card of their own, but can be made on the same cards dealing with the main subject. This method can be particularly useful where material is being passed over to the inactive files. In such cases it might be advisable to eliminate a heading and its corresponding cross-references, which can be done automatically if the above precaution has been taken.

12.7 WRITTEN RULES

Everything outlined in the present and previous chapters can be carried out with the utmost ease, if every company takes care to put the procedure into writing.

Until a short while ago, the files were the undisputed domain of a handful of specialists, who committed the whole procedure to memory. When these people were absent, the company was in grave trouble because the filing service was paralysed.

Nowadays it is not conceivable to leave such an important function at the mercy of an employee. Well thought-out procedures are needed and each phase must be made into a written rule. Only in this way can the efficiency of the filing depend upon the type of system adopted and not upon people, who can then be replaced or temporarily substituted without too many difficulties arising. Training of new personnel will be facilitated and, more important, this very important service will not be isolated in an ivory tower, but accessible to all members of the company.

13

DOCUMENT MOVEMENTS AND CONTROLS

13.1 EFFICIENCY OF THE SERVICE

The efficiency of a semi-active file is determined in equal measure by the speed and accuracy with which the folders reach the desk of the person wishing to consult them and by the frequency with which requests are made.

A semi-active file weighed down by useless papers and documents is usually inefficient. It may therefore be useful to test its functionality from time to time. To this effect we have established some pointers which give a pretty clear idea of the actual state of affairs.

The first pointer is this:

$$\frac{\text{Number of documents requested every year}}{\text{Number of documents filed}}$$

It is concerned with the movement of the documents in the files and, in order to indicate a satisfactory situation, it should be about 10%. Below this limit, it is obvious that too much useless material is weighing down the service and the files should be pruned.

The second pointed is concerned with the organization of the files:

$$\frac{\text{Number of untraced documents}}{\text{Number of documents sought}}$$

If this pointer is below 0·3%, all is well. If it is above 0·3%, the whole organization must urgently be gone over and a number of controls set up to avoid the excessive loss of material.

13.2 CONTROLS

The question of controls is one which deserves to be gone into carefully, since it is well known that too many controls militate against the functionality of the service. It must not be forgotten that, in the final event, it may be more convenient to risk losing some documents rather than weight down the semi-active files with useless red tape.

In a structure such as we have outlined, controls of the semi-active files must be as simple as possible. In the first place, everyone should have access to the material filed, the only limitation being that no document should be removed without the responsible filing clerk having made a note of the fact. Consequently, documents should be loaned without formality, either following a telephone request, collection by an office boy or the party concerned.

Special attention must therefore be given to the movement of the papers, since no loan should evade control. There are two reasons for this: it is the only way statistically to record the movements and there is no other way of containing the loss of documents within reasonable limits.

Control can be exercised by inserting a card, as in Fig. 13.1 in place of a document removed from a file. Such cards can be reused

J. Brown & Co.		Documents out of the files		
Secretariat				
Date of loan	Heading	Subject	Date received	Date returned

Fig. 13.1 Facsimile of a card to put in the place of a loaned document

several times, since at least twenty entries can be made on them, it being understood that the last entry made is the valid one.

Should a complete folder be removed, it is advisable to put a similar folder clearly marked 'OUT' in its place. This procedure has a double aim: to make it quite clear that a folder is missing (the name of the person borrowing it will be written outside the substitute folder) and to enable fresh material to be stored in it until the folder borrowed is returned (Fig. 13.2).

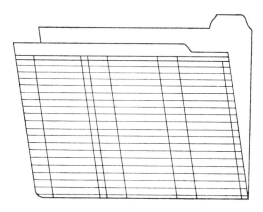

Fig. 13.2 Insert for file out on loan

Obviously, the risk of documents getting lost is greater when whole files rather than individual papers are borrowed. Since it is absurd to expect the filing clerk to check every paper in a folder before giving it out on loan, the only way to limit the risk is to limit cases in which a complete file is given out on loan.

In spite of all precautions, however, the possibility of a document getting lost still exists. As soon as it is realized that a document is missing, an attempt should be made to reconstruct it, partly from memory, partly from other documents, etc. When this work has been done, the new document should be marked 'Original document lost' and inserted in place of the lost one.

The cards inserted in the place of a loaned document are the only means of knowing how much traffic there has been in the files and they should therefore not be destroyed. In the better organized offices the inward and outward movements of documents are counted and the resulting figures are used for the compilation of statistics serving to demonstrate the efficiency of the service, as mentioned briefly at the beginning of this chapter.

13.3   DOCUMENTS ON LOAN FROM THE FILES PASSED FROM ONE PERSON TO ANOTHER

In order to avoid the loss of documents, it is necessary to establish which is the most suitable procedure to follow when documents are given out on loan to one person, who then passes them on to another. In theory, the problem can be solved by holding responsible the person actually borrowing the document from the files. In practice, however, this is too general a rule to be workable. Some companies therefore lay down the rule that material to be passed on to others should first of all be returned to the files. This procedure, however, can cause unnecessary time to be wasted and it is therefore better to lay down a definite rule requiring a person who hands over a document to another, to make a note of the fact and inform the filing clerk, who will in turn make a note of it on the appropriate card. In this way a document can pass from one person to another without the intervention of the filing clerk, who is none the less informed of the various movements.

Obviously, this system requires the willing co-operation of all offices, for it is sufficient for one employee to frequently forget to pass on the message to the filing clerk for the whole system to collapse.

13.4   OTHER CAUSES OF BREAK-DOWN

The need to control the activities of the semi-active files is not limited to the movement of the papers, however. It covers the whole of the system, which can break down for several reasons:

A classification system which is unsuited to the real needs of the company.

The absence of written rules on the daily procedure to follow so that the papers are transferred regularly, and on the loan of documents and, in general, services rendered to third parties.

Incorrect location of the semi-active files with respect to those using them more frequently.

Equipment which is not perfectly suitable for practical classification and easy access.

The absence of a suitable organization and adequate controls
for passing material from the active files to the semi-active and
inactive files.

Inexact or badly written indications of the content of files.

Poor lighting and ventilation.

Overloaded equipment.

13.5   CONTROLLING THE INACTIVE FILES

A great deal of what has been said with regard to controls of the
semi-active files is also valid for the inactive files. In this latter case,
however, there is no need to control the relationship between
documents preserved and those borrowed, since the main object of
the inactive file is to preserve documents until they lose all legal or
operative value. Controlling the movement of documents remains a
live issue, however, and loaning out documents will occupy a great
deal of the inactive filing clerk's time.

Here too efficiency demands that requests for documents be filled
as quickly as possible. However, this principle will frequently be
hampered by the fact that inactive files are located at some distance
from the central offices.

This limitation of a logistic nature makes it necessary to establish
with absolute precision when the various documents can be passed
on to it, so that requests for consultation of material in the inactive
files are quite exceptional and tend to satisfy interests of a historical
nature. Otherwise the efficient working of the business would run
into a new obstacle not easily overcome and would unquestionably
suffer.

The logistic location of the inactive files also imposes a particular
discipline in filling requests for consultation of documents. It is
advisable, for instance, that people request documents direct and in
writing (with very few exceptions). For their part, the people in
charge of the inactive files should deliver all documents requested at
the end of the day or at established times, depending on the distance
separating the inactive files room from the main building.

Otherwise, the same rules apply as for the semi-active files.

As for the length of time a document can be given on loan, this will depend upon the reason for the loan. The normal loan period, however, will vary between ten days and a fortnight. The most advisable procedure, none the less, is to loan the document for ten days, subject to renewal for a further ten days, if requested. It is a good rule for the filing clerk in charge of loans to send a list of documents overdue to top management at regular intervals, together with the names of the borrowers. If this is not done with some regularity, it is not inconceivable for some of the material to get lost, particularly in view of the fact that loans from the inactive files consist mainly of whole folders or dossiers.

13.6 PHOTOCOPIES AS A MEANS OF AVOIDING LOANS

As we have seen, the fear of losing documents prompts the use of procedures—sometimes quite costly—to regulate the requests for loans and their granting. Furthermore, the filing clerks need a certain amount of time to refile the documents loaned, as well as periodically to check which material is on loan and remind laggards to return it.

For these reasons there is a case for not loaning the original documents, but photocopies, which are destroyed after use. The recent advances made in photocopying techniques, which now make it a very simple and inexpensive process, together with the constant increase in the cost of personnel, suggest the timeliness of looking into this process and comparing it with the traditional procedure, in all cases in which it is technically possible, or economically convenient.

In practice, for papers which can be photocopied, the degree of economic convenience will be determined by:

> The number of sheets comprising the document to be loaned. If there is one sheet only, then a photocopy is unquestionably to be recommended. If many sheets are involved, it is very doubtful whether photocopying would be worthwhile.

> The time required by the procedure of loan, return, checking, and reminders and the savings in time made possible by the new system (it normally takes between 5 and 10 min. per loan). The type of apparatus used for photocopying. (There is a

considerable difference in price and efficiency between the various machines on the market.) If photocopying is considered, then a flat-bed machine that will copy from books or bound files should be used.

The importance of the documents being loaned and the amount of risk one is willing to take on their going astray.

Once it has been decided in principle to adopt this system, careful preliminary studies must be made and precise rules laid down on when to loan photocopies and when the original documents.

14
OBSOLESCENCE

14.1 THE NEED FOR PERIODIC ELIMINATION OF FILED DOCUMENTS

We have frequently made the point that the files must not only preserve, but above all, produce the documents requested at the right moment.

We have also pointed out that the probability of a document having to be examined tends to diminish as time goes by and after a while becomes almost nil.

It follows quite clearly that it would be absurd, both from the economical and the functional points of view, to want to preserve everything for an indeterminate length of time and in the same place. On the other hand, it must not be thought that the problem of pruning the files can be solved by arranging for all papers which have lost their operative value to be destroyed.

A certain gradualness is needed before a document passes from the hands of its compiler to the waste paper basket. This necessity is taken care of by the sub-division of the files into active, semi-active, and inactive, as we have seen. The existence of these three levels of filing means that the problem of thinning the busiest files (active and semi-active) is a real one. In fact it is an indispensable premise to the better functioning of the whole system.

The thinning-out process is carried out by regularly transferring documents from the active files to the semi-active files and from the semi-active files to the inactive files, before destruction. What remains to be seen is how these transfers can be carried out within the framework of an exact organizational plan.

There are two methods:

Transferring files at fixed intervals.
Continuous transference of files.

14.2 TRANSFERRING FILES AT FIXED INTERVALS

The first method is usually followed for transferring material from the semi-active files to the inactive ones. It consists in periodically removing all documents dated before a given date. This operation is usually carried out every year and results in the files losing a quarter, one-third or even half of its papers, according to how far back one goes.

If, for instance, there are 40 filing cabinets with four drawers each, that is, approximately 120 linear yards of filing space, and if it is supposed that documents increase at the rate of 40 yards a year, it is obvious that only papers pertaining to the current year and the two preceding ones can be preserved. This gives us a total of three years. At the beginning of every year, therefore, all papers filed two years previously will have to be eliminated.

If this method is followed, an increase in the material to be filed does not necessarily mean an increase in filing equipment, since there is nothing to prevent the papers from being transferred more frequently. It is hardly necessary to add that this statement is valid only insofar as it does not interfere with the proper running of the semi-active files. The opposite can be the case, with the same limitations, in the event of the amount of material diminishing.

14.3 CONTINUOUS TRANSFERENCE OF FILES

The second method calls for the material to be transferred with a certain frequency: daily, weekly or, at most, monthly. This method is most suitable for the active files.

It is not advisable for the semi-active files, because if transfers are made at the frequencies mentioned, it is not possible, for obvious reasons, to go through every folder and the temptation is there to thin out only the more voluminous ones. In such cases thin folders would be allowed to stay put almost indefinitely and in the long run they would be a hindrance to the semi-active files and no one would think of putting a remedy to the situation.

The warning not to use the continuous-transfer method for the semi-active files is given because this method unquestionably has some very interesting aspects:

It eliminates heavy seasonal work, and substitutes a habit which becomes integrated with the current work.

The filing cabinets are always full and therefore maximum use is made of the equipment.

A space economy of around 10% is made.

Not only the oldest documents are transferred to the inactive files, but also less interesting ones, or those which have lost their 'active' interest.

To gain these advantages one can follow the continuous-transfer method for the semi-active files, on the condition that transfers are also made at fixed intervals. In such cases the fixed intervals can be longer—every five years, for instance.

In such cases it is especially important for continuous transfer to be carried out according to well established rules indicating precisely when each document must be transferred. This method will reduce the possibility of 'personal' interpretations diminishing the efficiency of the system.

In the case of the active files, continuous transfer is the optimal solution, inasmuch as it is the only way to prevent the papers from lying dormant for too long in the drawers of the original users.

14.4 TRANSFERRING DOCUMENTS FROM ONE FILE TO ANOTHER

14.4.1   TRANSFER FROM THE ACTIVE TO THE SEMI-ACTIVE FILES

Special care must be given to the organization of the transfer of papers from one level of filing to the next.

The first phase of the transfer process begins in the active files. We shall therefore begin our investigation at this point.

The active files are merely a transitory depository for the documents. According to the purpose we have given them, documents should not remain in them for a period longer than that required to perform on them the most urgent actions. It is therefore necessary for everyone who has in his charge an active file to undertake regularly and continuously to sort the documents which have been entrusted to him.

The best guarantee that this is being done is for the rules which every company must have on transferring files to be followed. Such rules must first of all regulate the frequency with which papers are sent to the semi-active files.

A week is definitely an average interval which can be advised in the majority of cases. However, other intervals can be fixed according to the particular needs of a business.

The essential thing is that on the established day each work station sends on to the person in charge of the semi-active files all documents which have lost their 'active' function. Another rule which should be followed is for all offices sharing the same set of active files should transfer material on a different day, so that the filing clerk does not have too large a work load.

A decision should be made in each individual case as to whether transfers should be made without any formality or whether they should be accompanied by a checking form. The first solution should be chosen in smaller offices, where an excess of red tape only results in useless cumbersomeness. The second solution is to be recommended in larger companies. In such cases, the form shown in Fig. 14.1 is recommended.

In order to facilitate the filing, it is furthermore advisable for the senders to divide the material into the appropriate classifications, sorting it into the appropriate order. This will simplify the work of the clerk in charge of the semi-active files, who will simply have to merge and file the various groups of documents.

14.4.2 TRANSFER FROM THE SEMI-ACTIVE TO THE INACTIVE FILES

Transfers from the semi-active files are usually carried out periodically—preferably once a year.

Before beginning the work the filing clerk responsible must provide himself with all the necessary material: large containers, cardboard boxes, etc.

When the transfer day arrives, the filing clerk should begin the work methodically by examining the papers in the filing cabinets. In order to facilitate the work, the material in each individual folder should already be segregated by year in appropriate card files. The work will therefore simply boil down to taking out the oldest of the interior files, which should be clearly labelled and year-dated.

As for the choice of equipment in which to store the material to be sent to the inactive files, it should be considered in relation to the nature of the documents comprising each unit to be filed. If it is expected that the material will have to be referred to fairly frequently, at least initially, then easily accessible equipment should be chosen

XYZ COMPANY

LIST OF DOCUMENTS SENT TO THE SEMI-ACTIVE FILES

Department (1) . . . . .   Sending office (2). . . . .

Date (3) . . . .

Nature of the document (4)	Date of document (5)	Length of semi-active preservation (6)	Notes (7)

Signature . . . .

Fig. 14.1 The numbered references on the form have the following meanings:
(2) Indicate office or name of person effecting the transfer. (3) Date of transfer.
(4) Give a succinct description of the document. (5) Give date of emission of
document. (6) State how long the document must be conserved in the semi-active
files and whether it should then be destroyed or passed on to the inactive files.
(7) Indicate any filing anomalies.

This form is usually made out in duplicate: one copy remaining with the
sender as proof that the document in question has been properly transferred and
the other copy going to the person in charge of the semi-active files.

(suspended files). If, on the other hand, it is anticipated that the
material will hardly ever need to be referred to during the whole

period of its preservation, then larger containers (cardboard boxes) should be selected. When making the choice it should be borne in mind that the unit of material transferred to the inactive files should

FILING LABEL	
Issuing	Division .... Office .... Department .... Section ....
Year in which documents were issued	19 .....
CONTENT (give as detailed information as possible)	
TO BE DESTROYED IN 19	
	Section reserved for the files
Stick label here with reference number	

Fig. 14.2   The filing label contains the following information: the department issuing it; the year it is made out; the content of the box; the year of destruction. If one container includes documents issued in various years, it is the most recent year which is taken into consideration when fixing the date of destruction. The label is stuck onto the visible side of the container.

XYZ COMPANY | Serial No. (5) . . .

LIST OF DOCUMENTS SENT TO THE INACTIVE FILES

Department sending material (1) . . . . Date of despatch . . .

Name of person to whom list must be returned (2)

Reference No. (3)	Nature of documents (4)	Destruction date	Space for filing department

Fig. 14.3. The numbered references on the form have the following meaning: (1) Specify whether administration, sales, production, etc. (2) Give the name of the sender. (3) Give the number of the container enclosing the documents in order to facilitate the filing clerk's work. (4) Give contents of each container: if necessary, use more than one line for each unit enclosed. (5) Give the number which the unit of contents has been given by the filing department. (We suggest using adhesive labels numbered in quadruplicate: one copy is stuck to the unit in question, the second on the filing label (see Fig. 14.2), the third in the arrival book and the fourth in the destruction book.

This form is used, first of all, as a delivery note to accompany the material sent to the inactive files. It is then returned to the office which sent the material, marked with the location of the material. Properly perforated and carefully filed, it enables the semi-active files to give a location number on every request for material from the inactive files.

also be the unit preserved in the latter. To this effect, each unit transferred should be labelled (see Fig. 14.2) as to contents, e.g. 'Customer correspondence, 1960, Able to Courtney'.

Each transfer should be accompanied by a delivery note, in duplicate, giving the details of each unit transferred to the inactive files (see Fig. 14.3).

The transfer en masse of all the folders to the inactive files without any previous sorting, can result in uselessly cluttering up the files, since many papers can be destroyed before the transfer is made. In order to facilitate sorting, we suggest marking the papers to be eliminated in the top right-hand corner (preferably with a coloured pencil). Here is a list of documents which should not be transferred to the inactive files:

Covering letters without their enclosures.

Requests for information without their enclosures.

Letters, memoranda, and postal cards of simple information.

Requests for information and corresponding replies not requiring any action of an administrative character, decisions of an exceptional nature or elaboration of particular points.

Various communications to peripheral offices which do not require the carrying out of any administrative act.

Correspondence relative to invitations to meetings and functions (invitations, confirmations, refusals, various agreements, sending of aide-mémoires, etc.), with the exception of final motions, minutes, and orders of the day.

Notes and correspondence relative to modifications to mailing lists and indexes, with the exception of the actual guides.

Shipping lists.

Correspondence and internal memoranda relative to company organization (e.g. requests for printed matter, agreements on visits or trips, temporary working regulations, etc.).

Correspondence regarding publications in the course of production.

Bulletins, communications, notices, etc. from public and private organizations, of a purely informative nature and in no way official.

Notes approving proofs.

Internal memoranda regarding the forwarding of copies, photographs, duplicates, graphs, and tables of exclusively internal use.

I

Statistical data sent by specialized organizations and subsequently published officially.

Documents relative to various requests for charities not connected in any way with the activities of the business.

Applications for employment, negative replies, letters asking candidates to come in for interview, etc.

Various papers regarding the staff (doctor's certificates regarding sick leave, requests for leave, formal correspondence, etc.).

Letters announcing the arrival of official documents or explaining their content.

Correspondence relating to unimportant requests of various sorts to branches or agencies.

Follow-up letters of various sorts sent to outlying offices or received from head office.

Observations, notes, aide-mémoires and similar annotations regarding ordinary matters which did not progress further.

Requests for advertising material, letters ordering books, magazines, etc.

Once all the material has arrived at destination it can be bound rather than stacked away in containers (as previously suggested). Binding is advisable both because of its low cost and the space-saving it permits. This type of binding is usually done with a very simple machine which permits the papers to be gathered together and then presses them between two cardboard covers of the desired size. The contents of the volumes can then be written on their spine.

Once bound, the papers are permanently secured.

14.4.3   HOW LONG TO PRESERVE DOCUMENTS IN THE INACTIVE FILES

The length of preservation of the inactive files must be clearly established beforehand and indicated on the form accompanying the material, so that it is completely outside the influence of the filing clerks. It is a problem which should be solved when the classification and filing systems are decided upon.

In carrying out this investigation it is advisable to bear in mind that documents are not only important from the taxation point of view, but also from the documentary point of view in connection with the history and development of the business. It follows that not only book-keeping documents, invoices, contracts, etc. must be preserved for a long time, but also papers regarding production, personnel, sales organization, etc. which could be useful for documentary purposes in the event of an award of some sort, a special concession and so forth.

We therefore advise taking such matters into consideration, as well as current legal regulations, and statistical experience when deciding how long to preserve documents. A fairly simple way to find out how frequently documents in the inactive files are called for is to make an accurate note of every request. This will establish that the majority of requests (approximately 90%) are for documents which have been filed for less than six months, while little more than 1–2% of requests will be for documents filed for more than two years.

The rule which can be deduced from what we have so far set down is this: it is well to set a fairly long period for the preservation of papers, without however being exaggeratedly cautious. According to a study in depth carried out in a number of companies, it turned out that their respective files could have been thinned out by at least 35% without harm.

While the classification system is being evolved, it should not be forgotten that, initially, many documents are filed in more than one copy. Such is the case with invoices, for instance, which are usually made out in several copies, which go to various offices for different purposes (statistical, accounting, etc.), in addition to the copy which is kept in numerical order as required by law. It is obvious that after two years at the outside, the one copy filed in numerical order will suffice for every use. In the case of more important papers, it is advisable to file duplicates, in different places, of course.

We should add that corridors and the various locations of the inactive filing cabinets should be appropriately identified by a number or a code, so that every section is easily distinguished.

Destruction of the papers should be carried out according to the order laid down in the register mentioned in chapter 12.

It is best actually to destroy the papers rather than to sell them as old paper. The papers should only be sold after being cut up finely with the special machines which are now widely used. In the absence of such equipment, burning is the best solution.

Sometimes before a document is destroyed its main details are registered in a book, but we feel this is excessive, at least in the majority of cases, and a pure and simple waste of time.

15
THE 'ACTIVE' FUNCTIONS OF THE FILES

15.1 THE FILING SYSTEM AS AN ACTIVE MANAGEMENT TOOL

The semi-active files are the work centre of the whole filing system. Within the framework thus far outlined, the semi-active files have co-ordinating and controlling functions within that complex function which includes the classification and preservation of the documents.

The modern business is an organized complex of people and things in continuous evolution. The services which make it up must therefore be quite dynamic in order to respond to the changing needs which continuously arise. The files cannot be an exception to this rule, since they constitute one of the most important tools through which management can achieve its objectives.

15.2 ENSURING THE CORRECT FUNCTIONING OF THE SYSTEM

This postulated, let us see which are the main functions of the semi-active files. The most important one is obviously that of collecting, classifying, and preserving the material. There are other functions, however, which have already been referred to and which are by no means secondary. Briefly, they are:

Making sure that material is sent to them at regular intervals by the various active files.

Making sure that the classification details marked on the documents by the various people in charge of active files are correct.

Filling requests for documents held by the semi-active files.

Speedy forwarding of requests to consult material filed in the inactive files.

Checking the length of loans and, if necessary, urging borrowers to return overdue documents.

Sorting and filing material to be sent to the inactive files after thinning out the semi-active files.

It will be noted that all the above functions are extremely important to the satisfactory working of the filing system. If they are neglected or omitted one of the most delicate departments of the business will be paralysed and the groundwork will be laid for disorder in all the other departments of the business.

15.3 THE FUNCTION OF THE SEMI-ACTIVE FILES VIS-À-VIS THE ACTIVE FILES

The semi-active files exercise a pre-eminent controlling function over the active files. Their aim is to make sure that papers do not 'idle' for too long in the drawers of the various employees, holding up the work of others. The clerk in charge of the semi-active files should therefore prod all employees who originally receive documents so that they do not hold them for any longer than necessary and hand them over regularly at the appointed dates.

Another of the semi-active files' task is to loan out all documents requested and to make sure none of them is retained over the allotted time without justification. The clerk should enter all loans in an appropriate register, as this is the only way to keep track of loans and to follow up on overdue documents.

With the filing clerk's permission loan periods should be renewable, when necessary.

The efficiency of the filing system can be demonstrated in practice by the speed with which documents requested reach the hands of the people concerned.

To this end it is advisable to do away with all formalities, permitting anyone to have any paper he needs at any time. A phone call, a written request, the sending of an office boy—are all valid means of securing a needed document. The only formality which should not be omitted, as we have already mentioned, is for each request to be entered in a register, complete with details of the document and of the person borrowing it. (Obviously, this applies only if the original document is loaned and not a photocopy.)

These entries will also prove extremely useful in determining what changes may need to be made to the classification and filing systems. The data gathered from the register will in fact make it possible to ascertain whether the length of time for which documents are kept

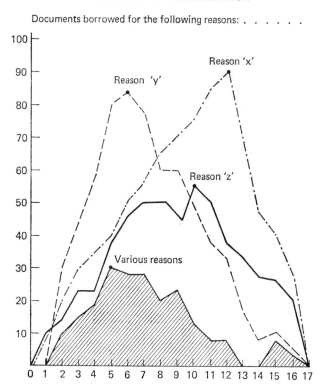

FREQUENCY OF CONSULTATION

Fig. 15.1 The statistics worked out by those responsible for the files can easily be put into graphs. The graph illustrated shows the various reasons for which documents were borrowed.

in the semi-active files conforms to requirements, or whether it is excessive or not long enough (see Fig. 15.1).

Finally, it is the task of the semi-active files to check up on the work carried out by those in charge of the active files. The documents reach the semi-active files already prepared to be filed in the cabinets. It would be wrong, however, to trust blindly to the classification marks on them. The clerk in charge of the semi-active files should check these marks and make sure they conform to the classification plan in force in the company, make any necessary modifications, and then file the document according to the final classification which he decides is most appropriate. Only in this way is it possible to be absolutely certain that papers are not mislaid in classifications not actually included in the plan.

15.4 THE FUNCTION OF THE SEMI-ACTIVE FILES VIS-À-VIS THE INACTIVE FILES

As we know, documents spend most time in the inactive files. In their journey through time, which lasts on average some fifteen years and during which papers start off in the active files and end up in the incinerator, the longest pause is made in the antechamber to destruction, i.e. the inactive file. Here they have above all a historical value, even though they may still be loaned out. Documents must none the less be filed with absolute precision, permitting quick retrieval when needed.

The function of the semi-active file vis-à-vis the inactive file is well defined and leaves absolutely no room for doubt. Its task is to prepare the material so that all the clerk in charge of the inactive files has only to place it on the appropriate shelves. All the papers must be collected in the order agreed upon and put into the containers where they are to remain until destruction. These containers can be of different types, as we have already seen, i.e. cardboard boxes, folders and so on. The choice will obviously depend upon how accessible the material needs to be, which, in turn, will depend upon how frequently it is anticipated that it will need to be consulted. At the outside, the only task which may be left to the inactive files is that of binding the material received, but without changing its order. The problem of accessibility must be carefully considered, because the request for a document will mean sending the whole unit, apart from exceptional cases. The semi-active files will also have to give the inactive files all instructions regarding preservation, including duration and importance, all of which will be indicated on the delivery note with the material. A copy of these delivery notes will be retained by the semi-active files and will be referred to each time material needs to be consulted.

15.5   THE REGISTER

The semi-active files can also be entrusted with a task which, at the first sight, may appear to be extraneous to its main activity, but which actually has all the qualifications to form an integral part of it. We refer to the register.

The intense activity which is carried out in an office frequently results in the staff having difficulty in remembering things which are

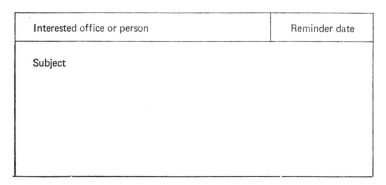

Fig. 15.2   Example of card for the reminder register

not of a repetitive nature. For this reason it is advisable to assign the task of 'remembering' to a centralized system—the semi-active file. In effect only the file is able methodically to collect all the material and remind the interested parties of it at the appropriate time, passing to them all documents, notes, aide-mémoires, etc. as they become due for action.

The main method for the systematic organization of such a task consists in filing the material by due date. The person concerned tells his secretary or himself marks on an appropriate card (Fig. 15.2) the date on which he wishes to be reminded of a certain matter. The clerk in charge of the semi-active files integrates these cards with all the necessary material, sorts them into chronological order, and puts them in a box, with markers to divide each working day in the month. If the traffic is not very great, it may be possible to have a marker every five days only.

If the due date is marked on the document itself, then the filing clerk will have to transfer it to a card and file the document from which he has got the information in the regular files.

Every day the clerk will take out the cards due the following morning and send them to the offices concerned, together with the pertinent documents from the files.

This register, complete with date divider cards should cover, at most, a period of two months. It should be brought up to date automatically: that is, when all cards pertaining to a given date are taken out, the date marker should be moved forward to the corresponding place three months hence. If it should happen that certain cards have to be removed before the register has reached the date in question, they should be placed behind the marker for the appropriate month until such time as the marker for the day is moved forward.

16
THE COST OF FILING

16.1 BREAKDOWN OF FILING COSTS

We have already pointed out, in the course of the previous chapters, that classification and filing are activities which require staff, space and equipment, all of which cost money.

If we now want to analyse these costs further and see how they break down, it is advisable to single out the main motives of which they are the basis. Generally speaking, the cost of a filing system can be broken down into the following headings:

Decision to file.
Filing the document.
Transferral to file.
Filing.
Preservation of the document in the file.
Request for the document.
Retrieval of the document.
Waiting for the document.
Transmittal of document.
Consultation of document.
Slowing down of traffic.
Office floor space used for filing.
Filing equipment.
Equipment for transporting the documents.
Lighting, heating, air conditioning, etc. for the rooms used for the filing.
Accessories: boxes, cards, folders, forms and other reference cards, etc.

From this simple breakdown it becomes obvious—as we shall see more clearly further on—how strong a contribution to the cost is made by the movement of the staff; not only the filing staff, but also the staff making use of the filed material, who have to wait for it for shorter or longer periods, according to how well the filing system is organized. We have brought out this point right away to make it perfectly clear that the greatest savings in the cost of filings are to be made in the better use of personnel.

16.2 AN EXAMPLE OF COST CALCULATION

We are now faced with the problem of putting a value on the main groups into which we have broken down the cost. We may as well admit right from the start that the task is not an easy one and, at best, all we can do is make an estimate, leaving the individual companies to adapt the figures set down to their own particular needs. That is to say that it is impossible to work out a filing cost which could be adapted to every situation, since every point of departure is different. Let us therefore start off with some assumptions. Let us assume that the papers are filed in cabinets in alphabetical order. The office is situated in the City and the rent is around £5 per square foot. Papers are preserved for five years and an average of twenty are received each working day.

If we make these assumptions we can break down the total filing cost as follows:

1. Amortizement of filing cabinet (a four-drawer model has been selected, costing on average £60, plus another £60 for the suspended files. A useful economic duration of ten years is envisaged) £12

2. Rent, heating, etc. of the area occupied (4 sq. ft.) . .   £20

3. Filing clerk's work, calculated on the basis of 40 min. per day (in smaller offices a secretary can be given the task and her cost can be calculated at £0.01 per min., since her annual salary, including fringe benefits can be calculated at about £1200 . . . .   £100

4. Cost of time lost by the person requesting and making use of the document* (assuming the level of organization is satisfactory) £30

Annual cost £162

---

* The calculation has been worked out on the supposition that the person in question is worth £3000 a year, i.e. £12 a day, or £1·50 per hour. (£3000 divided into 250 working days equal £12. Assuming he devotes approximately 20 hours a year to the task in question, this gives us: hourly cost £1·50 × 20 hours equals £30.)

If 10 000 documents are classified in alphabetical order according to client (50 folders per drawer with an average of 50 documents each), the filing would cost more than £0.01½ (1½ new pence) per year per document. This is rather a high cost, in spite of the fact that the assumption that each folder would contain 50 documents is rather optimistic, since, generally speaking, the average is lower, and consequently the cost of filing goes up.

This figure reiterates the opinion, repeatedly expressed, that:

It is advisable to preserve only indispensable documents.

It is best to classify them as economically as possible and in such a way as to be able to retrieve them quickly and easily.

It follows that the first principle to be adhered to if filing costs are to be cut down or eliminated, is not to produce a document, if it is produced internally, or destroy it right away, if it originates outside. Obviously this is an extreme case and not always practicable. On the other hand, it is not unusual to find companies which make out useless extra copies of documents, which are then classified and filed, again to no useful purpose. In fact a little research turned up the fact that many companies keep a volume of documents from two to ten times greater than their needs. By cutting down on this volume, the companies concerned could save up to 20% of the space used and cut down their filing costs from 3 to 1.

From the above it can be deduced that the criterion regulating the filing—apart from legal or fiscal regulations, which are inescapable—should be: the total cost of filing must be less than the cost resulting from the absence of the document.

When the above-mentioned legal or fiscal regulations demand that a certain document of no operative value be preserved, then the classification system must provide for its immediate transmittal to the inactive files, which are far less costly to run, compared with the semi-active files to which these notes refer.

In an attempt to evelute the cost of the various headings into which the total has been broken down, we have confirmed the fact that the cost is mainly made up of personnel expenses, which account for 70–80% on average. Hence the need to select a filing system and filing equipment which can keep filing costs within reasonable limits.

As for the classification system, it should bear in mind ease of filing, but also take into proper consideration frequency of consultation and the need for requests for documents to be filed quickly.

If, for instance, chronological order is selected as the type of classification to be followed, filing time will be greatly reduced. Retrieval,
on the other hand, will take much longer. The opposite happens
when a geographical–alphabetical–chronological classification system
is adopted.

Before deciding on the classification system to adopt a company
must therefore consider the time factor: if it is anticipated that
documents will be needed with great frequency, then there is no
question that a very precise classification system should be chosen,
even if it is more costly at the filing stage.

The cost of personnel influences not only the choice of classification
system, but also the choice of equipment. The choice must be based
upon the same considerations outlined above.

Part III

CLASSIFICATION AND FILING EQUIPMENT

17
EQUIPMENT FOR ACTIVE AND SEMI-ACTIVE FILES

17.1 THE PRINCIPAL FILING SYSTEMS

Filing systems in a small business can be simple, usually with a straight alphabetic index, but as businesses grow, so does the need to file documents under more diverse headings. Also the various departments become more mechanized in their handling of paperwork and this in turn demands different filing and indexing methods.

For general correspondence in a small business, a manilla folder for each letter of the alphabet, and a box file with invoices or bills again filed in alphabetical order may be quite sufficient to locate any papers whilst they remain active.

One of the simplest ways to file these is to lay them flat on shelves (this method can also be used for large documents, plans, etc.), or placed horizontally in drawers.

For a larger business, a separate folder will be required for each company with whom business is regularly transacted, with a general or miscellaneous file for each letter of the alphabet.

These might be filed in filing cabinets and kept upright in the drawer by a 'pressure plate'. This is a sprung metal plate which slides in a metal carrier at the bottom of the drawer and a spring can be released to move it backwards and forwards. This is known as 'vertical' filing.

More modern methods have evolved files which have metal or nylon carrier bars across the edges and these are suspended on metal carriers in the drawers and are called 'suspended' filing.

This method has been used with various kinds of indexing.

One is called 'Tab filing' and has protruding tabs on each of the files, which are progressively positioned across the files to aid quick identification.

The second method is 'top-vision' where the front edge of the file has a plastic shield about $\frac{1}{4}$ inch wide into which is inserted a typed strip containing the name of the individual or company concerned. It is then possible to insert into the main file folders, separate folders say for various individuals in the one company.

These files can be individual, i.e. filed separately, or linked together by slotting into one another. The second method saves misfiling, but means that files have to be physically separated to insert a new file.

In addition to the traditional filing cabinet, which can now be obtained in 1, 2, 3, or 4 drawers high, suspended files can be hung on shelves or put into cupboards. These can be fitted with roller shutters or blinds, or have folding doors.

Therefore, markings must be on the ends of files which is known as 'lateral continuous' filing. Generally this type of file has a cut-away edge on which the name or tab is placed, but on high shelves, a method of indexing called 'vertical vision' is used which is similar to top-vision except that the name is now on the end of the file. Occasionally the angle can be variable according to users' requirements.

There are a number of variations on these basic methods according to the styles of each manufacturer and files can be placed in desk drawers, mobile trolleys (see Plate 5), or in portable carriers like attaché cases. These variations will be discussed in more detail in each of the sections to which their housing methods relate.

Whilst no guarantee is given as to completeness, a broad survey of filing methods available in Britain is given, but some companies have individual variations on a basic pattern.

17.2 FILES, FOLDERS, WALLETS, ETC.

The basic equipment for many filing systems is the manilla folder, but this can be obtained in a number of different forms, shapes and sizes (see Plates 1A–1F) and these containers can be stored in a variety of ways (e.g. see Plates 2 and 4).

A large number of manufacturers will supply the ordinary manilla folder, which can be 'square cut', both edges cut square, or 'tabbed', the rear edge with a tab protruding, usually in any one of five or six positions across the width of the folder. Many suppliers will also provide about five colours of cover to order.

In addition, folders can be punched to take thongs or laces, or be provided with metal or plastic prongs with various locking devices.

Some folders can be provided with fold-over flaps or gussets to act as wallets for unfileable items such as samples or thick catalogues.

Some files are expandable by a variety of folding methods or by fitting metal or plastic pillars which have two or three inches of filing capacity. Also expanding wallets can be made from manilla pockets gummed together and tab-indexed A to Z or 1 to 31 (see Plate 6). These are useful for sorting before filing, or for updating reminders. Modified versions of this type are available for domestic use (see Plate 3A).

Some binders also have spring clips or spring binders for loose-leaf filing.

Other types of files are those with stiff strawboard covers with spring clips or lever arch files, usually with A to Z indexes. There are also special files made up for legal documents, complete with pink tying tape and seven, eight, or nine part files for separating active documents for conferences, etc. There are also many special files which are variations of basic folders, or wallets, and storage wallets and cases which are described under equipment for inactive files. There are also the more unusual methods of circular lateral housing units, etc., which are described in more detail elsewhere.

17.3 FILES SUPPLIERS

Almost any retail or manufacturing stationer will be able to supply the basic manilla folders, as will the suppliers of filing cabinets. There are also a number of firms who will supply specials, but this does not imply that all suppliers named will do so.

17.4 HORIZONTAL OR FLAT FILING

This method of flat filing (see Plate 7) is particularly useful for large documents, plans, etc., but usually suffers because of the problem of proper indexing.

Where drawings or plans are prepared internally they can be allocated a sequential serial number and filed by this number, with a subject cross-index.

Where these are received from outside, frequently from several sources and on various subjects the problem is more difficult. It will depend on the need for reference as to how the items are filed. If they are always referred to by subject then file accordingly, separating by supplier or date, whichever is more important. If they are referred to by supplier then adopt this method, probably with a numerical index for each item received from each supplier.

Where items are bulky, or can be rolled up into long narrow items, then file in pigeon-hole shelves, racks, or bins. Some racks can be obtained with slotted dividers which permit quick removal or transference to take larger or smaller items. This method is frequently used in legal offices and also in works stores for items with incoming paperwork.

Some manufacturers will manufacture specialized shelving for this type of filing, and it is interesting to note here that in the Victoria Tower of the Houses of Parliament are special storage racks for the ancient 'scrolls' or records which have been kept for hundreds of years and the many volumes of parliamentary papers which are too bulky to keep in the usual library shelves, but to which reference is made by Members and Peers at fairly frequent intervals (see Plate 25A).

The disadvantage of this type of filing is that it takes up a large area and in many cases indexing and reference is difficult without lifting each item filed in the drawer or shelf to see the reference number or name.

With pigeon-holes or bins, the problem is that either many are not full and space must be left for future requirements or else all spaces are filled to capacity and it is pure chance that the document required is on the top of the pile.

For this reason, this type of filing is preferred for the inactive files.

17.5   VERTICAL FILING

Filing cabinets with compressor plates can be seen in many offices and are supplied when bulky files are likely to be used. They can be obtained in 1, 2, 3, 4 and occasionally 5 drawer heights in usually British Quarto (10×8 in.) and Foolscap (13×8 in.) internal drawer widths, although more use is being made now of A4, the International Standard paper size which is approximately $11\frac{3}{4} \times 8\frac{1}{4}$ in. Tabbed files are usually used, although stiff guide cards can be inserted between sections.

Vertical filing is also a favourite method for accounting machine ledgers which can be stored in trays and moved to and from the operator on a mobile trolley and filed in fireproof cabinets. The method of indexing is usually alphabetical, although numerical or alphanumeric could be just as suitable in some circumstances. This is also described under card-filing methods.

This type of filing has been modified for plan and drawing filing, with corrugated dividers between each section keeping drawings filed vertically, with a consequent saving in floor space. There is also a spring-loaded planfile with different sized concertina pockets, into which small or large plans are placed and kept upright by spring pressure.

This equipment is shown in Plates 8 and 10.

17.6 SUSPENSION FILING

As previously mentioned, suspended files probably account for more than 50% of the files used in Britain, mainly because a neatness and order can be introduced in suspended systems which is usually not possible in other methods.

Even plan filing, which is still traditionally either horizontal or vertical flat filing, has succumbed to suspension methods and several kinds of suspended planfiles are available.

This method is also used for filing stencils, offset plates and other items which often were unlikely to be considered suitable for filing and finding again (see Plate 9).

17.7 TAB FILING

One of the ways of signalling files is to use a metal or plastic tab which stands proud at the top of the file and into which can be slipped a typed name, or even just a letter or number.

For ease of reading these can be staggered across successive files or colour-coded by subjects or on particular files which will make them more easily indentifiable.

Alternatively, each letter of the alphabet can be given a different colour coding or the coloured signal tags used in card index systems can be used to identify important files.

Special indexes can also be obtained such as stock control or a salesmen's call system in a similar manner to card index systems.

Filing pockets can be single or linked together and many now have nylon inserts in the metal runners for quieter sliding (see Plate 11).

Where files are used by more than one person, a pretabbed 'OUT' file can be put in for any file removed and a note kept in the file as to the person using it.

This type of file, particularly the non-linked systems, can be transferred from main filing cabinets to desk drawers or to home filing units or back again at will.

17.8 TOP-VISION FILING

Whenever filing systems are displayed at exhibitions there is always a large amount of 'top-vision' filing, since this looks extremely neat, especially so if the present system in an office is a poorly kept vertical system.

Address slips can be arranged in a number of patterns so as to make indexing and classification easier. For instance, with an alphabetic file, the main letter divisions can be to the extreme left, names of individuals or companies in the centre and miscellaneous labels on the extreme right.

Colour coding can also be used, either for each letter or section or to divide one section from another and coloured metal guide bars can be obtained so that these, combined with coloured paper or plastic title strips, can give a wide range of colour combinations.

Again special combinations of alpha and numeric, or numeric, say for date reminders 1–31, or subject filing can be arranged. Geographic or geographic and numeric can all be put in easily as these types of files lend themselves to easy identification and tabs do not become broken off.

If colour-coding for each letter of the alphabet or number is used, it is easy to spot a misfile.

Again, use should be made of 'OUT' files and many companies use a manilla folder or duplicated card which is placed in the file giving the date, name and department of the person to whom the file is on loan.

Plates 12 and 13 show some top-vision equipment.

17.9 LATERAL FILING

Lateral filing can be suspended on shelves, in cupboards and in a number of other ways to take advantage of the space saving obtained by this method. As files are placed endways, shelves or cupboards need only be approximately 13–14 inches deep and six or seven rows in height can be used.

Some units have a front and rear rail onto which files are hung, others have a central, hook-on rail of T or H section on which files slide.

Cupboards can be fitted with an aluminium roller shutter, canvas or plastic blind which slides down the front channels of the cupboard and locks at the bottom. Alternatively, single or double folding or quarter slide-away doors can be fitted to cupboards for space saving.

There are also special cupboards where files lie diagonally on rails so that they appear like top-vision files filed sideways. This system incorporates a plastic file carrier and each title strip is visible from the front.

This type of filing is also available in self-contained 4 ft sections which fit one above the other and alongside each other in the diagonal fashion. Units can be placed one above the other and slid across from side to side to reach the bottom units, as shown in Plate 13.

Lateral shelf filing can also be static or mobile on castors or sliding rails to save floor space and some shelving units have motorized bases to save the manual effort of moving them.

A pull-out reference tray at working height can also be fitted to shelving to enable papers to be sorted before filing. Shelves can be fitted with front beading into which index names or letters can be fitted.

Cupboards and shelving can also be obtained with a mixture of lateral, card index and box filing for small offices where filing space is at a premium (see Plate 23).

Lateral files can also be suspended in desk drawers, in a separate filing pedestal attached to a desk or in mobile trolleys and personal filing boxes.

Some equipment is shown in Plate 14A.

17.10 VERTICAL VISION FILING

This is one of several variations on the lateral systems in which files have the identification running vertically instead of at an angle.

Some systems have a variable angle of indexing so that lower shelves can be tilted at a different angle to higher ones, as shown in Plate 14B.

17.11 MISCELLANEOUS FILES

As previously mentioned there are a number of variations on the standard.

In both suspended and lateral files it is possible to obtain bulk pockets for filing large quantities of documents or bulky catalogues, etc.

It is also possible to get double entry pockets to enable filing to be reached from either side, so that the shelving can be used as an office divider.

Also special long files can be obtained for stencils, litho plates or X-ray films and special wide files to take 18×14 in. documents such as medical cards, etc.

Expandable files for varying amounts of current information such as orders or seasonal records and files with posts or pillars for continuous stationery and other marginally punched documents.

There is also a form of 'lateral shelf filing' where the pockets are not suspended, but are made semi-rigid to stand upright of their own accord. Shelf dividers are used in shelving rows to keep these files from falling over.

Nor are items to be filed solely documents. Samples, tools, dentures, shoe lasts, chemical compounds, very often with supporting paperwork require filing while awaiting attention or despatch, and usually bins or shelving is used to accommodate them.

There are also many special systems for filing accounting records in books, trays and binders which vary very little from card index filing and can be found under that chapter.

Finally there are various rotary methods for filing box files, suspended or lateral files which are claimed to save floor space over most other methods.

18
EQUIPMENT FOR INACTIVE FILES

Care should be taken that inactive files are just that. If correspondence or other documents are taken from active files or semi-active too frequently, then storage files which are being kept for record purposes or for statutory reasons become semi-active and most equipment used for inactive files does not lend itself to easy reference of individual papers.

On the other hand the active filing system should not be cluttered up with material which is obviously inactive.

The problem comes in deciding exactly when to thin out files, as discussed in chapters 8 and 11.

Having decided that the time has come, but the material must be kept in case of future queries, then documents should be put in transfer binders or box files (see Plate 15A). These can be made of thick paper, manilla, strawboard, metal, or plastic, but whichever kind is chosen it should be capable of being handled easily and indexed clearly. Some material lends itself to binding into book form, complete with hard covers, but much will be stored in boxes or cases.

They should then be stored, preferably on metal shelving rigidly secured to a wall, as many office juniors have an unfortunate habit of climbing up the front of filing shelves to reach the top shelf without always using a step-ladder.

There are, however, other items which have to be kept, such as printing blocks, samples of materials, etc., which might be better stored in bins or even in flat drawers. This applies particularly to drawings or plans which are filed this way in the active files and might suffer damage by other filing methods.

18.1 SHELVING

The type of shelving used for storage can be purchased from a number of suppliers and is usually supplied with adjustable shelves not less than 8 inches and not more than 12 inches deep.

Widths vary from 24 to 48 inches wide, with the average at 36 inches, but care should be taken on wider shelves that they are strong enough to take the dead weight of filed paper, or are reinforced accordingly.

Heights are dependant on space available but care should be taken not to stand single bays of shelving over six feet high without top or side support (see Plate 15B).

18.2   POSITIONING OF SHELVES

Shelving should be positioned in a reasonably dry atmosphere as paper quickly absorbs moisture and some of the chemical 'no carbon required' and other copy papers lose the colour of their image in damp conditions. In fact, some papers can have the image removed by water.

Other types of imaging are affected by heat, such as the heat or infra-red process photocopies, and papers of this type stored alongside radiators or near a boilerhouse would turn black and no readable image would remain.

Heat and damp also have an effect on several other kinds of photocopies, especially if the developing salts remain on the paper, so for archival storage, reflex and diffusion-transfer copies should be washed in the same way as photographs in running water.

Strong sunlight will also fade ink, ballpoint or pencil used for marking covers and colours used for indexing, so ideally storage shelves should be in a dry, windowless room which is not too warm. Records which must be preserved indefinitely, such as State papers, are stored in air-conditioned rooms.

18.3   FIRE PRECAUTIONS

As paper is obviously highly inflammable, strict fire precautions and a 'No Smoking' rule should be observed in the non-active file area. A fire escape should be provided from the area and whilst water will damage any stored records, a sprinkler system might well be worth the investment to save the major portion of records before a fire can get a hold, or if storage is below a working area.

18.4 BINDING EQUIPMENT

When transferring from current files it is frequently easier to stick to the current method of securing papers into the files than to invent a new method.

Where papers are loose, then some form of binding equipment, which might be a spring clip in a box file, or manilla folders with a sprung spine, or even pillar or post binding files for continuous stationery should be used. Otherwise papers become misplaced easily if reference is made to them and future reference becomes impossible. Book-binding equipment using plastic fasteners is also now available and can be used by the office junior.

18.5 INDEXING

When transferring, the outer case of the transfer binder should be suitably titled. It may be sufficient to index with one or more letters of the alphabet and the date from and to, for any correspondence (see Fig. 14.2).

In the case of copy invoices or works orders, etc., a numerical sequence may be possible.

Or subject, geographic or other indexing methods should be used which reflect the main active and semi-active filing methods.

Also a note should be made in non-active files as to where any previous correspondence can be located to save hours of fruitless searching.

10.6 DOCUMENT-DESTRUCTION APPARATUS

When inactive files have ceased their useful life they should be disposed of, but many companies are loathe to part with them intact in view of the danger of industrial and trade secrets being divulged.

Therefore, some method of disposal must be found.

Some companies go to the trouble of burning all old files in an incinerator, but this can be a slow, costly and sometimes dangerous business unless the right location and weather conditions are chosen.

Other firms dispose of their old files for waste paper, but take the precaution of shredding the paper beforehand (see Plate 16).

Shredders can be obtained in all sizes from a small, office model which will take single sheets of paper to a heavy duty model which could dispose of a complete file, a box file complete with strawboard folders or even single metal litho plates used in offices for offset printing.

In between these two extremes is a variety of other models of different capacities.

19
CARD-INDEX FILING EQUIPMENT

Not all information received in a business can or needs to be filed in a manilla folder. It may be only temporarily current information such as the receipt of goods into a business. Their arrival has to be posted somewhere and their use also noted. Therefore, some form of card-index record is sufficient to record movement of stock in and out, or for sales or maintenance records where information is posted from some other source.

Card indexes can also be used for cross-reference indexes to main files for employees' records, for customers' names and addresses, for telephone numbers and many other internal records.

Therefore, the two main types of uses for cards are as posted records or as indexes.

Cards are available in a wide range of sizes, with standards at 5×3, 6×4, 8×5 and 9×6 inches, but a number of non-standard sizes are available for special uses such as an $8 \times 5\frac{1}{2}$ in. for tax-deduction cards. Also cards can be obtained in ready perforated sheets to make tear-off strips after typing which are filed into special holders.

Records in a sheet form can be obtained with a variety of rulings to suit purchase and sales records, stock, costs, wages and so on. These are filed in special binders, some with the records staggered to present a visible edge for each sheet.

There are also cards where the information is not written down but punched into a series of holes, either internally into the card or along the edge where the information can be retrieved by mechanical or electronic sorting.

As with other filing methods cards and sheets can be filed in a variety of ways. These are usually vertical or horizontal, blind or visible edges, in drawers, boxes, or trays.

19.1   VERTICAL FILING

Card-filing drawers can be obtained in single units or multiples in cardboard, wood, or metal. These can sometimes be attached together in stacks or in complete cabinets. Two- and four-drawer cabinets are also made with top depressions to enable other cabinets to be located on top. Drawers can be obtained which take two, three, or four rows of cards alongside each other with dividers in between (see Plate 17).

Cards are filed in alphabetical or numerical order with tabbed guide cards at suitable intervals. A wide range of sub-divisions of the alphabet can be obtained ranging from a 24 tab to 40, 80, 120, 240, or 500 sub-divisions of various letters such as Aa to Ad, Ae to Aq, Ar to Az, etc. For heavy-duty work, metal-edged tab cards can be obtained.

Tabs on cards can be obtained in various cuts. Fifth cut means that five different positions across the top of the card can be obtained. Also available are third cut, half cut, and specials from some suppliers.

For library uses a number of preprinted tab cards for month or date, biography, fiction authors, and so on can be supplied.

Numeric sub-divisions can also be obtained from several suppliers from stock, particularly 1–31, but special printings are usually available on request.

Blank tabs can also be obtained to enable your own system of indexing to be entered, or with plain plastic containers for a written or typed slip to be inserted.

Cards can also be obtained either blank or feint ruled and with a number of standard rulings for stock records, purchase or sales records and so forth. Also special rulings are available from most suppliers.

Cards can also be supplied with rulings across the 5-inch dimension of a 5×3 card, or across the 3-inch way and drawers are available accordingly. The most popular size for this is 8×5 or 5×8 card filing sizes.

19.2   VERTICAL MACHINE ACCOUNTING FILES

Ledger cards used in machine accounting are frequently filed in posting trays with an alpha or numeric index very similar to standard vertical card filing.

Some companies also make a visible edge card which have cut-outs at the bottom to enable the cards to be located in echelon. The cards are filed in an overlapping arrangement with an index or reference on a top right-hand corner which is cut diagonally. The cards locate from left to right in order in the filing drawer and the removal of one card can be noticed by a gap in the sequencing.

19.3 ROTARY VERTICAL FILING

Loose cards with tabbed indexes can also be filed in rotary housing units (see Plate 18A). The cards are not punched or attached in any way but are kept in place by a system of belts and pulleys which keep the cards in their housing by the tension of the belts and only those cards in the top 10 or 12 inches of space are open for selection.

Depending on the size of the cards, the number of compartments on each wheel of the rotator is varied. Typical spacing would be 40 compartments for 3-inch-high cards, 28 for 4-inch-high or 20 for 5-inch-high cards.

Cabinets can be obtained with from one to five wheels in width, although various permutations of card width and wheel width can be arranged.

Typical capacities for a one-wheel unit would be about 7000 5×3 cards or about 6000 8×5 cards, but some units can be obtained which are smaller or larger than this. To estimate filing requirements allow about 100 cards per inch of filing space.

It will be seen from this that in one rotary unit, 50 000 cards or more can be filed thus allowing one operator access to more cards in a smaller area than the average desk unit.

There are several variations on this basic pattern.

There are also several rotary systems available where the bottom of the card is punched with a hole or a keyhole edge punch to allow cards to be filed on carrier rods.

19.4 ROTARY HORIZONTAL FILING

In addition to the above units where the cards rotate vertically, there are also filing units into which cards can be filed to rotate horizontally on a series of circular filing shelves (see Plate 18B). A typical unit would file about 12 500 cards size 5×3 on one wheel of 27 inches diameter.

19.5   HORIZONTAL FILING

The majority of horizontal filing methods for cards and sheets are nowadays visible edge methods with one card or sheet overlapping on another to allow for the card title to be located quickly (see Plate 19).

Cards can be housed either in a pocket with a plastic edge at the bottom, or cards can be suspended on a rail or carrier by clips and other methods.

Card housing units can be cabinets with 6, 8, 12, or more trays on slides per cabinet, or they can be housed in book units, desk units or even wall housing units. The numbers of cards per slide varies according to the maker and can be from 50 to nearly 100, with 72 being about the average.

Card sizes can be the regular 5×3, 6×4 or 8×5 although this type of unit favours larger cards and several makers stock units to take 13×6, 11×9, 12×8 and other sizes.

Also the amount of edge visibility can be varied, with $\frac{3}{16}$ inch or $\frac{1}{4}$ inch being the usual.

Because of these variations, the capacity of units of the same size can vary considerably and some makers supply what are known as 'duplex' units where two small cards can be housed side by side in the same tray.

Continuation sheets which are more flimsy than the original card can also be used and some units carry these flimsies as standard.

Flimsy sheets are also the basis of a wide number of accounting systems where data are posted onto loose-leaf visible records held in book form. Wages, material and stock control, purchase and sales records are all available as standard rulings.

These and other visible-edge cards lend themselves to edge signalling with metal, plastic or coloured paper indicators. Some company's methods include several variations such as slip on, stick on, sliding, or sliding telescopic signals, in from four to at least a dozen different colours. Also printed signals with letters or numbers can be obtained in various colour combinations, or holes can be punched in a signal as required. Cards can be obtained also in a number of different colours for different purposes to aid codification.

19.6   STRIP INDEXING

Where a limited amount of information is required quickly, such as

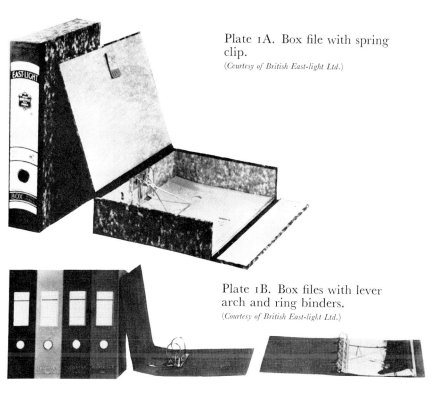

Plate 1A. Box file with spring clip.
(*Courtesy of British East-light Ltd.*)

Plate 1B. Box files with lever arch and ring binders.
(*Courtesy of British East-light Ltd.*)

Plate 1C. Manilla folders with ring binders.
(*Courtesy of British East-light Ltd.*)

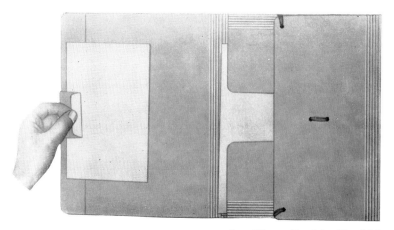

above Plate 1D. Manilla folders
with spring clip and gussets for
loose papers.
(*Courtesy of British East-light Ltd.*)

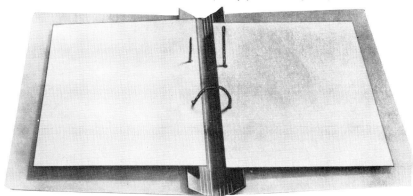

above Plate 1E. Spring thong
binders in a manilla folder.
(*Courtesy of British East-light Ltd.*)

below Plate 1F. Storage case
which can be used for loose
papers or files.
(*Courtesy of British East-light Ltd.*)

above Plate 2. Circular file
store for lever-arch files
or ring binders.
(Courtesy of Expandex Ltd.)

right Plate 3. A
personal home file.
(Courtesy of Twinlock Ltd.)

above Plate 4. Suspended filing using manilla folders inside.

(*Courtesy of G. A. Harvey Ltd.*)

right Plate 5. Mobile filing trolley for both suspended tab files and box files.

(*Courtesy of Western Trading Co. Ltd.*)

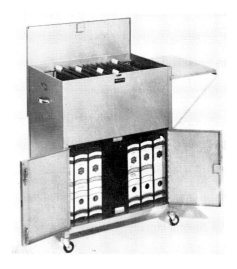

right Plate 6.
A to Z filing
wallet.
(*Courtesy of British East-light Ltd.*)

below Plate 7. Flat plan filing cabinet in wood.
(*Courtesy of Abbot Bros. (Southall) Ltd.*)

above Plate 8. Vertical plan filing cabinet.
(*Courtesy of Art Metal*)

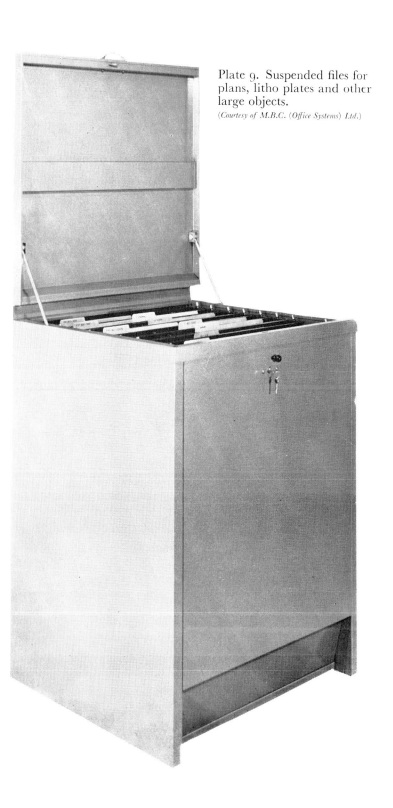

Plate 9. Suspended files for plans, litho plates and other large objects.

(*Courtesy of M.B.C. (Office Systems) Ltd.*)

left Plate 10.
Mobile accounts
card trolley.
*(Courtesy of Western Trading
Co. Ltd.)*

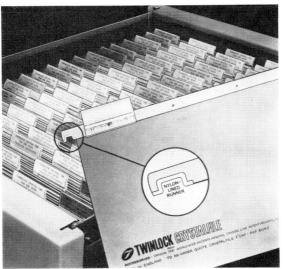

left Plate 11.
Tabbed suspen-
sion files with
nylon-lined
runners.
(Courtesy of Twinlock Ltd

above Plate 12. Flat-top suspended filing
with coloured signals.
(*Courtesy of Shannon Ltd.*)

left Plate 13.
Anson 'Vistapack'
filing unit with
4 ft mobile sections
which can be
moved across for
access to the lower
tier of files.
(*Courtesy of George Anson
& Co. Ltd.*)

above Plate 14B. Vertical-vision filing in folding-door cabinet.

(*Courtesy of Frank Wilson (Filing) Ltd.*)

opposite Plate 14A. Suspended lateral filing with different indexing methods in a roller-shutter cabinet.

(*Courtesy of Roneo Vickers Ltd.*)

left Plate 15A. Transfer case.
(Courtesy of Trade Loose Leaf Co.)

below Plate 15B. Steel shelving showing trans cases in position.
(Courtesy of The Welconstruct Co. Ltd.)

below Plate 16. Paper-shredding machine.
(Courtesy of Ofrex Ltd.)

left Plate 17.
Large-drawer
card-index
cabinet which
can be divided
centrally to tak
two sets of card

(Courtesy of Roneo Vickers Ltd.)

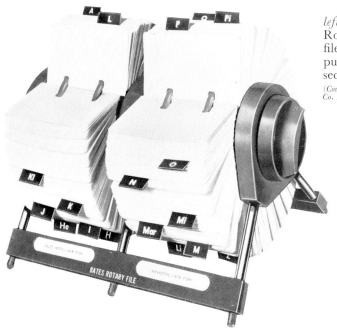

left Plate 18A. Rotary card-index file with cards punched for security.
(Courtesy of Magowan & Co. Ltd.)

below Plate 18B. Rotary horizontal filing equipment.
(Courtesy of Rotadex Ltd.)

above Plate 19. Multi-tray visible index cards, showing pull-down, lockable front.

(*Courtesy of Copeland Chatterson Ltd.*)

below Plate 20. Rotary strip index stand.

(*Courtesy of Art Metal*)

above Plate 21A. 'Findex' punched-card system with vertical hole punching.
(*Courtesy of C. W. Cave & Co. Ltd.*)

left Plate 21B. 'Findex' sorter showing the required cards off-set after sorting.
(*Courtesy of C. W. Cave & Co. Ltd.*)

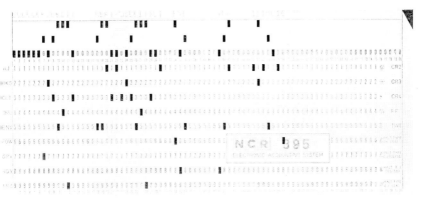

above Plate 22. Typical punched card.
(Courtesy of N.C.R.)

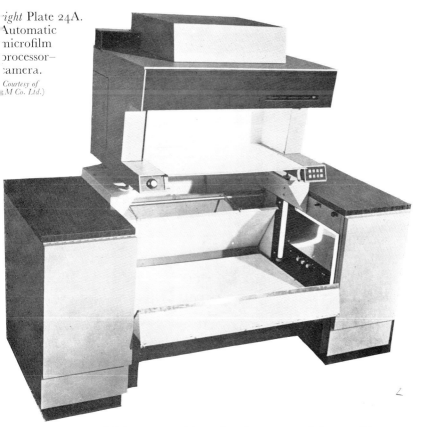

right Plate 24A.
Automatic
microfilm
processor–
camera.
*Courtesy of
M Co. Ltd.)*

opposite Plate 23. Multi-storage cabinet showing many of the possible
filing combinations.
(Courtesy of Intercraft Designs Ltd.)

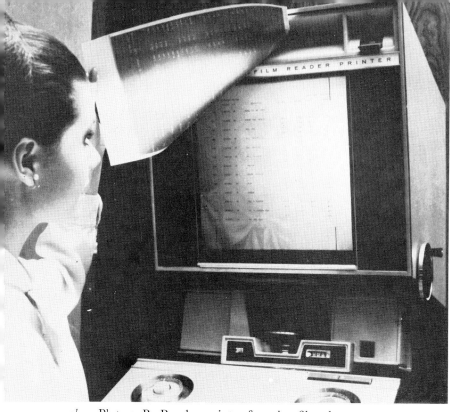

above Plate 24B. Reader–printer for microfilmed pages.
(*Courtesy of 3M Co. Ltd.*)

below Plate 25A. Filing shelves for historical records in Victoria Tower, Houses of Parliament.
(*Crown copyright. Courtesy of Ministry Public Building and Works*)

above Plate 25B. Railex Rotomatic mobile files.
(Courtesy of Frank Wilson (Filing) Ltd.)

below Plate 26. Remington Lektriever.
(Courtesy of Remington Rand Division of Sperry Rand Ltd.)

above Plate 27. Remington Remstar.
(*Courtesy of Remington Rand Division of Sperry Rand Ltd.*)

above Plate 28. Varimaster filing unit fitted
with shelves to take data-processing
material.

(*Courtesy of Sankey Sheldon Ltd.*)

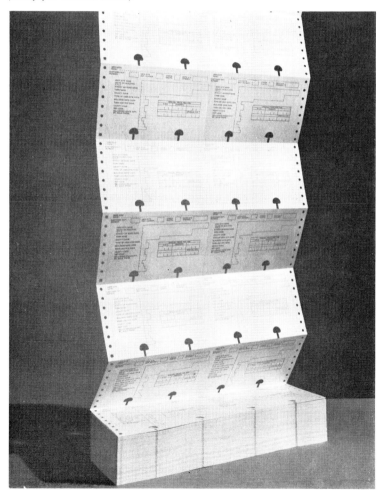

below Plate 29. Continuous printed cardwheel cards for rapid print-out from a computer.

(Courtesy of C. W. Cave & Co. Ltd.)

the name, address and telephone number of a supplier or customer, then a blind index is slow to locate and a visible page index is wasteful unless the page is filled with other information which is static. If the page is filled, or any information is altered the whole lot needs retyping.

Therefore, for telephone numbers, cross-reference indexes to numerical or subject files, alphabetic to geographic indexes and so on, a strip index is used. Depending on the type required, one, two or three lines of typing can be accommodated and strips fixed into single- or double-sided wall panels, rotary and desk stands, folders, and books (see Plate 20).

Widths can vary from about $\frac{3}{16}$ to $\frac{3}{4}$ inch and strip lengths from 4 to 10 inches. Panel lengths are from 12 to 25 inches so that capacities are extremely varied.

Coloured signals can also be attached in a similar manner to some card indexes.

19.7 PUNCHED-CARD MARGINAL PUNCHING

In order to save valuable time in posting information and finding it again, data-processing methods have evolved which put information onto a card by means of a hole or a notch. Used in a predetermined area, this will signify information of one kind or another. This is of a 'go' or 'no-go' type of reference.

For instance, if these cards were used for staff records, a slot in area 1 would indicate male and in area 2 female, so that when the cards are sorted manually by passing a steel rod through the holes, a rod inserted into area 1 and then raised would leave behind all the slotted cards, i.e. male cards.

Additional slots can be punched for various information on all four edges if required, and for easy identification, say for job or clock cards, hand written or typed information can be added into the central area.

Various sizes of cards and kinds of punching can be used for different systems, and coloured cards can be used to identify different subjects to be indexed.

Another system of a similar sort uses large cards which have not only edge punches but also internal slotting to indicate various codings (see Plate 21A). Retrieval is carried out by putting all the cards into a selector frame, putting one or more selecting rods

L

through the relevant holes in the front and rear of the frame, then, when the frame is turned sideways cards slotted in the appropriate places will fall down $\frac{1}{2}$ inch (see Plate 21B). Cards can then be counted. The use of several rods at the same time can make retrieval more selective.

19.8 PUNCHED CARDS FOR TABULATORS AND COMPUTERS

This subject can only be briefly introduced here as it is a subject on which much can be said. However, more mechanical means of filing and finding information were required by businesses and Herman Hollerith invented his method of coding a card way back in 1890.

Several other kinds of similar cards are, or have been in use, but modern equipment has been standardized on the 80-column card (see Plate 22).

This card has 12 punching positions from the top to the bottom of the card and 80 punching positions along its length. For easy identification to see that a card is the right way up, the top right-hand corner is cut off.

The card is printed from 0 to 9 and holes punched in these areas are known as 'digit punches'. IBM cards use a rectangular hole, Remington cards a circular one, and so on.

In a position above the 0 a hole can be punched in what is known as the '11 or X punch' hole and above this again the '12 punch' hole.

The key factor for punching and retrieving the information is the location of the hole and IBM have designated certain positions to the numbers, letters of the alphabet and special characters as found on a typewriter keyboard. One, two, or three holes punched in these designated areas will be sorted as that particular number or letter.

Therefore, these specific columns allocated are called fields. The unallocated columns, say 1–8, 19–26 and so on can be allocated to one or more fields for further information to be punched according to the system in use.

If we use the method described in marginal punched cards, column 1 could be allocated to male and column 2 to female. Holes punched in column one, digits 0 and 1 could signify 'male, under 18'. In digit 0 and 2 'male, age 18–21' and so on. These first two columns in a personnel system could be designated as the 'sex and age' file.

Other fields could be used to designate other characteristics, wage rates, etc.

These cards are punched by special key-punching machines, and after verifying that the correct information has in fact been put in, are stored in trays.

No particular order need be observed as when information is required, these cards are run through a mechanical sorter. The speeds of sorting these cards range from about 400 to 3000 cards per minute, although even faster sorters are now coming into use.

Cards are placed into a feed hopper, then fed through the reading section and sorted into bins according to the selection required. Cards are fed through sideways with the 9 or bottom edge first and the sorter has a metal roller, over which the cards pass and a reading brush above it.

When the card passes through, the column-selector switch positions the reading brush over one particular column, say column 20. Cards with a hole in column 20 can be fed into bin number 1 as the reading brush touches the metal roller through the hole, whilst all other cards go through to bin number 13, the reject bin.

In practise up to 12 selections can be made to speed up sorting, but to get one specific piece of information, such as 'How many males, age 18–21, earned more than £50 bonus on job number 27467?', may require several passes of the cards through the sorter.

It will be appreciated that this mechanical method of information retrieval is usually many times faster and less fallible than manual methods.

There are of course, many variations on this theme, and data processing has its own information storage and retrieval problems which can only be briefly considered here.

L*

Part IV
LOOKING TOWARDS THE FUTURE

20
FUTURE PROSPECTS

20.1 CURRENT TRENDS

The information given so far pre-supposes that the original data contained in each document is manually processed or only partially processed by automatic machines. Such methods fit into a management structure of the traditional type in which various departments form largely autonomous structures, each with its own management with well-defined responsibilities and authority.

This is why the files are sub-divided into three levels of activity. The active files being required for current use and for additions, analysis, extraction and so on; the semi-active are there to support and control for auditing and other management purposes; and the inactive for the need to preserve any historical, fiscal, or legal documents necessary to the company.

However, the present trend is towards more automation of company records by the use of automatic book-keeping machines, by data processing, and more and more by computers.

Therefore, the office is receiving and producing different kinds of information which require storing in different ways to the traditional methods.

20.2 THE MANAGEMENT 'FACTORY'

Instead of receiving information, invoices, bills, etc. and processing them through for a monthly or even yearly analysis, today's office is becoming an automated factory for the production of daily management information.

It is no longer possible for a business executive to 'fly by the seat of his pants'—in other words to run a business by 'feel' or even common sense. It is necessary as business becomes more complex to have facts readily and promptly available on which decisions can be based with more certainty than guess-work.

However, these facts can only be produced from the information flowing into or out of the company he runs and methods must be found of obtaining, processing, and disseminating these facts.

Also facts must be up-to-date if decision making is to be correct and timely, so processing of the data must be done as rapidly as possible.

20.3   INTEGRATION INTO THE ORGANIZATION

There is no point in processing data rapidly unless it can be used, and it is, therefore, necessary in many cases to re-examine both the organization and the structure of a company if and when mechanization is introduced.

The methods of processing and storing information by manual means are not necessarily suitable for use with mechanized processing.

The methods of handling filing will require revision as the shape and design of the input and output data will have altered in many ways.

This in turn will inevitably lead to re-assessing the personnel handling the data as some changes may be required.

Even the management methods of handling data will require re-examination as it is no use producing streams of facts daily, if the Board of directors or senior executives are only going to look at them once a week.

20.4   MECHANIZATION

Therefore, it may be necessary to introduce mechanization by stages. Only certain procedures in individual departments need be mechanized and the machines incorporated into an existing organizational structure without too much modification to the flow of work.

The other method is to introduce mechanization and modify the internal organization to adapt to it. This method is very often necessary when a company introduces computers into data processing, without managements being aware of it beforehand. It is for this reason that computers get a bad name for causing chaos, as a company attempts to adapt computer systems to an existing organization rather than adapting the organization to the system.

There may well be advantages or disadvantages in either method adopted. A smaller company may benefit from partial mechanization, a larger company from a more complete changeover.

20.5   CONSEQUENCES ON A FILING SYSTEM

In any case, there is likely to be some transformation in the filing methods, and as we move towards a completely automated office, it is reasonable to think in terms of automating the filing.

The problem is still one of storage, and whilst computers and other data processing methods have magnetic files capable of storing millions of words, storage of any and every piece of data on a magnetic file becomes a very expensive business.

Therefore, a variety of other methods of storage (e.g. that shown in Plate 23), or even of automating traditional storage and filing methods, is very often a more economical proposition than it may at first appear. It will depend very much on the nature of the item to be filed, on the accessibility required and on the speed required for processing it, or even the amount of reference required after the initial processing.

The next two chapters investigate the possibilities in more depth.

21
MICROFILM

21.1 POSSIBLE APPLICATIONS

One way of reducing storage space is to miniaturize the items to be filed, and reductions of 90% in the area required to store equal amounts of information are by no means uncommon. In fact, in some special systems it is possible to compress some 3000 pages of data onto one sheet of approximately 6×4 inches of film.

However, the saving of space is not the only advantage gained. Others are:

1 As film can be copied easily, an extra copy of a file can be used for security purposes, using one copy for active use and storing a second copy or in some cases, the originals, in other premises.

2 Obtaining copies for several departments to use or have access to the same material at the same time.

3 Diazo and similar methods of copying films produce cheap copies for use by sub-contractors, branches, overseas agents, etc., saving postage and larger copy costs.

4 By avoiding access to originals, particularly plans and drawings, these do not become damaged, necessitating expensive re-drawing and replacement.

5 With general correspondence, this can be destroyed after microfilming, so saving filing space.*

6 By using special systems, which will be described later, it is possible to speed up or mechanize the retrieval of data.

Microfilm has some disadvantage, not the least of which has been the refusal by makers of the equipment to tailor it to the smaller or more general requirements of an office. Other disadvantages are:

* It should be noted, however, that at the time of writing, the legality of microfilmed documents, especially as evidence in Courts, is still not fully accepted, although there is a Bill before Parliament which may alter this.

1 Most equipment to date has been made for one specific application by a large user (usually American) and the manufacturer
has tried to sell this same equipment for other uses.

2 Although this situation is changing, there is still much unsuitable equipment or perhaps equipment without sufficient
popular appeal for microfilm to become widely accepted.

3 Many prospective users have no clear idea how they might use
microfilm and have tried to put everything onto film at once.

4 Microfilm systems are only as good as the indexing, and many
systems fail because of inadequate or unsuitable indexing.

21.2   SYSTEMS

It may not generally be realized that microfilm was first discovered
in 1839 by J. B. Dancer, an Englishman who experimented with it in
his optical business and produced microphotographs (as film was not
then invented) within a few months of Daguerre announcing his
photographic methods.

Although some microfilming was carried out in Britain during the
19th century, it was adopted more by American business and since
the early 1900s has been widely used by a number of different trades.

Because of this a number of different methods of microfilming
have been used and different formats of film have been adopted; in
many cases because that particular size or gauge of film was available.

Reels of film usually 100ft long have been used in 8, Super 8,
9·5, 16, and 35mm, with 70mm and even 105mm in use at various
times.

Film has also been cut into strips, put into transparent jackets, or
cut into single frames and mounted into data-processing cards.
Whilst a popular format is a 35mm film in a standard 80 column
punched card with an aperture cut into it and known, therefore, as
an 'aperture card', at least 20 different variations of this are or have
been available at some time or another.

Also sheet film has been used with a sheet approximately 6×4
inches (148×105mm) in size being a popular format. This sheet
which is called 'microfiche' has 60 images of 16mm film size on it
when the card has a typed or printed reference heading, or 72
images (arranged in 6 rows of 12) when used as a continuation sheet.

However, other sizes of sheets have also been used, with 5×3 and
8×5 sizes following card-index formats among many others. Also

strips of 16mm film have been stuck to an acetate film base in the 60 or 72 image format to make a form of microfiche.

Where reference only is required there have been several systems which have used the opaque print-out from microfilm, as contact strips or in cards of 6 × 4 inches and other sizes as a library deck of cards. These are usually called 'micro-opaques'.

Also as previously mentioned, copying film (of silver halide quality) onto diazo film is cheaper, sometimes by as much as 50%. A proprietary brand of diazo type film called 'Kalvar' is also used for this.

Therefore, as microfilm for business systems use did not seriously get off the ground in Britain before about 1928 when Kodak set up their 'Recordak' division here, a wide variety of methods and systems has led to confusion in prospective users minds and many have failed to buy because the company they approached did not have the system or equipment which was right for their job.

21.3 EQUIPMENT

Because of the wide variety of systems there is a huge range of equipment on the market, and only by investigating the proposed application thoroughly can the right equipment be chosen.

For this reason it is not proposed to go too deeply into the methods and operations of equipment, but a brief outline is given for information purposes.

21.3.1 CAMERAS

In order to film the data, some type of camera must be used, although it does not follow that this will look anything like the popular idea of a camera used by the average photographer. However, most have a lens, a shutter and a variable exposure device to expose the film.

The two main types of camera are the 'planetary' and 'flow'.

The planetary as its name suggests takes pictures in the plan view, and in its simplest form could be a 35mm popular camera mounted on a column, above a baseboard onto which floodlights are shining. The item to be filmed is laid on the baseboard and according to its size the camera is raised or lowered so that the image approximately fills the frame of the film, the exposure calculated and the picture taken. The film is then wound on and the next picture taken until the the whole film is used.

There are, of course, more automated versions where the whole operation from deciding the ratio of the original to picture size, the exposure control, taking the picture and winding on the film, are all automatic from the touch of a button (see Plate 24A).

The flow camera is a continuous operation camera which can operate at quite high speeds, where the movement of the film is synchronized to the movements of the original and, therefore, photographs separate pages or continuous rolls of originals as required. This type of camera is very suitable for the microfilming of data from computer and other continuous stationery without separating the pages.

There are also special cameras for microfiche, but these tend to be very complex and, therefore, expensive pieces of equipment which can only be justified by high throughput.

21.3.2   FILM DEVELOPMENT

For the smaller user, the development of exposed microfilm is usually a matter of returning it after exposure for processing to the manufacturer of the camera equipment or a microfilm service unit.

When a user reaches a sufficient quantity of microfilm uses, it may be worth using any photographic film developing facilities within the company or buying a film processing unit. To be economical in use these need to be used to a fair degree and one film a day would certainly not justify obtaining such a unit.

As capital and running costs vary considerably according to the make, each company should make its own investigation of these machines before buying.

21.3.3   READING OR READER–PRINTER EQUIPMENT

Viewing of processed films is usually by means of a reader unit where the individual frame of the microfilm is enlarged back to life size, sometimes even larger, sometimes smaller, depending on the size of the original and the viewer magnification (see Plate 24B).

As there are various formats and kinds of microfilm there are also various reading devices, some to take roll film, some for single frames, some for microfiche. Occasionally one reader will accept several formats or can be adapted to take them.

In a number of cases there may be an occasional need to produce an enlarged copy from the microfilm for reference or for checking queries (in invoices, etc.). Sometimes this need is more than occasional, perhaps by a sub-contractor receiving working drawings from the originator and where several copies are required for workshop use.

In these cases a reader unit, equipped with a print-out device to produce hard copy is used. There are pieces of equipment which will enlarge to six or eight different ratios from various film formats and produce dyeline copies within seconds. In the microfilm business almost any item of equipment can be obtained if the need is there and the money with which to buy it.

It is, therefore, possible to buy cameras which will film both sides of a document at once, or can copy from bound books—and turn the pages—or readers which are portable and readers which can be viewed by remote control or by television.

21.4 INDEXING AND CLASSIFICATION

As with filing, a microfilm system is only as good as its index and a certain amount of pre-classification of originals or pre-sorting before filming is necessary.

21.4.1 NUMERICAL

With some systems, such as the microfilming of invoices prepared internally, it is only necessary to pre-sort these into numerical order to have sufficient index for future reference, as a customer can be asked for the invoice number in the case of queries.

This type of filming is best carried out on rolls of film which can film invoices in numerical order. These are then stored in cans in an outer cover which is indexed with the first and last numbers of the invoices filmed, and if necessary for reference the dates of the first and last items can also be shown.

There are a number of other items in a business where numerical classification is sufficient identification.

21.4.2 DATE ORDER

It is also possible in certain businesses where the amount of incoming information each day is quite large, but easily identifiable as to subject matter, to use a simple classification by date.

Each subject is sorted into date order and filmed on separate films or alternatively one film which is then cut into strips according to subject and filed in date order.

21.4.3   INDIVIDUAL

Where information comes into a business as one complete page, such as a plan or drawing, or where such information is prepared internally, there could be several departments that need to refer to this information for various purposes.

Also some departments may have different indexing or reference requirements to others, so unless a central registry is set up with a complete card index system, this information cannot be readily disseminated unless microfilmed and put into aperture cards.

These cards, as previously mentioned usually containing one frame of 35mm in an 80 column card, can have up to 50 columns of data punched into the card, which will allow for automatic sorting into subject categories on a normal data handling card sorter.

This means that even if only one copy of each card is made, this can be indexed to suit 5 or 6 departments, but it would be easier in many cases to make extra copies so that each department with a large usage can have its own set of aperture cards.

21.4.4   COMPANY

Where information is received regularly from companies, such as sales literature, brochures, price lists, etc., there is much to be said for microfilming this information if only to reduce the bulk of keeping such records at least for a year. For buyers and others this can mean considerable extra space for filing and, therefore, overhead costs.

The easiest way is to put all the information from one company onto one microfiche card which, on a 6×4 inches card can contain 60 or 72 images or pages of information.

The problem here is that the step-and-repeat cameras used to place these images side by side in rows down the sheet of film are usually large, complex and expensive.

It is possible to get this done as a service but usually only if there is a considerable and continuing flow of work.

For this reason, companies who want to use this facility film their information on a 16mm camera and then stick the completed films in rows onto sheets of acetate film with a colourless film cement. There is also at least one company offering film jackets to place these films into, in rows in the same way.

21.4.5   PRODUCT

In the same way product information can be gathered together onto sheets of film and several companies in Britain are now offering a service of sheets of microfiche containing product information of interest to engineers and others.

Also at least one company is offering a specilized version of this using PCMI (Photo-Chromic Micro-Image) an NCR invention, where the image is reduced by two stages in special cameras so that 3000 images can be contained on one sheet of 6×4 inches film.

This must obviously have a special viewer to enlarge this image back to readable form, but this viewer is provided as part of the yearly service together with several hundred thousand pages of information.

The index to each sheet is usually contained on an alphabetical card which refers to a particular frame on a card by position and row number. For instance, if 'Microfilm' happens to be the product required, this could be found on card M, and the item, say 'Recordak Microstrip Reader, Model PGR' might be image 37 on row 12. Therefore, the full index reference number would be M3712.

There are other indexing methods in use with these systems.

21.4.6 DIRECTORY

Where the rapid retrieval of information is required to be kept in a directory form, perhaps as a name and address, or a customers credit record, account identification or similar information, then the Recordak Microstrip is one of several systems which can be used to locate this information quickly.

With the Recordak system, pages of information are recorded onto 16mm film which is then placed into a rigid plastic holder which takes 12 inches of film strip. These holders are individually indexed by a pre-determined set of letters and numbers, which enables the operator to select a particular holder and then set an index selector to display the particular page and line required.

21.4.7 GENERAL

There are many other methods of indexing and classification systems in microfilm methods, some of which are highly complex and automated, but most are variations on the several themes mentioned here.

However, microfilm in itself is no answer to a bad filing system, as the fault usually lies with the method and type of indexing used for reference, which can be equally poor in microfilm if the wrong method is used.

22
AUTOMATIC FILING

22.1 FROM TRADITIONAL TO AUTOMATIC FILING

The use of microfilm systems is only one method of altering traditional filing and this can range from simple to highly automated. For many businesses, this may not necessarily be the answer they seek towards filing automation owing to the nature of the input and output documentation of the company.

By the introduction of punched card systems, or visual card accounting methods, the nature and size of the data can be radically changed from what it was previously.

There may be much information which is still arriving in its traditional form, or is being processed by semi-automatic machines which still retains its format, such as a card index. Therefore, it becomes necessary to automate the method of indexing and retrieval rather than to change the method.

In this chapter we will look at a few ways of doing this although it must be made clear that this is not a fully comprehensive review of all methods as new ideas on this subject appear with quite frightening rapidity, each of which claims to make some other method obsolete.

22.1.1 MOBILE RACKS
Although this does not automate the actual filing method, one way of saving filing space is to put double sided storage racks, which can contain active lateral files or non-active box files onto mobile castors. These can be moved by a geared wheel, or even have a motor drive with push button action (see Plate 25B).

This can almost double the filing capacity in a large room as it eliminates unnecessary gangways.

22.1.2 LEKTRIEVER ONE
For more automated methods of filing, Remington Rand have

introduced the Lektriever One which stores lateral files on a con-
veyor belt which can rotate up and over in either direction (see
Plate 26). There are six different models with varying file capacities,
the largest units being able to store up to 160 000 records in a filing
space of 119½ inches high, 78 inches wide, and 53¼ inches deep.

The method of retrieval is to push a button to select the shelf of
filing required and then extract the particular file. Retrieval time is
claimed to be not more than 8 seconds on average for any one file.

There is a built-in safety device so that should a carelessly replaced
file, or the operator's hand, cross the path of the carrier, the electronic
eye shuts off the unit's power.

22.1.3   RANDTRIEVER

Remington Rand have also introduced a more fully automated
system which will cater for millions of records.

The operator sits at a console and issues electronic instructions to
the system which locates and delivers the particular file within
seconds. This system can, of course, be highly complex and no details
of pricing is available as it can be tailored to a users requirements.

22.1.4   REMSTAR

For use with a central registry system and to enable users to
obtain information quickly, Remington Rand also have the Remstar
system of remote television transmission of information (see Plate 27).

A user can telephone his request to the registry, where the
information is located on Lektriever or Kard-Veyer units, and, after
locating the file, the operator places the document into the transmission station and it can be viewed by one or more persons on the
remote monitors.

22.1.5   KARD-VEYER

Other Remington items are the Kard-Veyer and the Lektriever
III which are card-index versions of the automatic filing units.

There are a number of variations of the Kard-Veyer according to
the card size and capacity, but different units of 5×3 inches size
could store from 125 000 to 400 000 cards, but for 8×5 inches cards
this could be 50 000 to 180 000 cards.

The Lektriever III is a larger unit for more card records and with
much more push button sophistication.

22.1.6   OTHER ROTARY CARD INDEX UNITS

There are also several other automatic or semi-automatic rotary card index filing systems, among them the ICC Card-a-matic and the Super Starline sold by MBC Office Systems Limited.

There is, however, an increasing tendency for all manufacturers of filing equipment towards automation, either in the method of filing or retrieval and there is no doubt that this tendency will increase.

22.1.7   COMPUTER PROGRAMME FILES

The problem with computers is that, not only do these machines generate a lot of paper output, but they also need information files where details of programme specifications, record layouts, test data, etc., can be filed. Jetley's have been specializing in this field for some years and have produced a special programme file of a stout orange manilla cover with a spring arch make-or-break mechanism incorporating a simple compressor bar. Eight stout guide sheets are provided to separate the papers, the first sheet being printed with headings and divisions for recording purposes. At the back of the folder is a gusseted pocket for the storage of computer print-out paper and punched paper tape. Data-processing material can then be stored in special racks (see Plate 28).

22.1.8   PUNCHED CONTINUOUS STATIONERY

Print-out from computers and other mechanical data processing machines can also be difficult to handle, but one method which combines continuous output with traditional card filing methods such as card wheels is available (see Plate 29). Several firms make binders with metal or flexible nylon posts which can be slipped through the punched holes and secured by clips in the top cover.

Where more permanent filing is required, a sealing machine which clips off the nylon and turns the end over into a stud by heating and forming, makes a permanent binder between two stiff outer covers.

There is no doubt that automation will still see a growing market for filing products.

Appendix 1: Types of Files and Suppliers

Supplier	Box file	Horizontal flat/top	Vertical non-suspension	Suspen. tabbed	Suspen. flat/top	Suspen. lateral	Suspen. vertical vision	Rotating	Misc.
Abbott Bros. Ltd.		X							
Alpa Steel & Plastics									X
Geo. Anson & Co.				X		X	X		X
Art Metal		X	X	X	X	X	X	X	X
Baird & Tatlock Ltd.		X		X	X				X
British East-Light	X		X		X				X
F. C. Brown Steel Equip.		X				X			X
Roy Bulmer Ltd.	X		X	X	X	X			X
Carter-Parratt Ltd.									X
C. W. Cave & Co. Ltd.				X	X	X			X
Copeland-Chatterson Ltd.									X

Supplier	Box file	Horizontal flat/top	Vertical non-suspension	Suspen. tabbed	Suspen. flat/top	Suspen. lateral	Suspen. vertical vision	Rotating	Misc.
Henry Elwin Ltd.	X	X	X						X
Expandex Ltd.				X	X	X		X	X
Flexiform Ltd.		Vertical sus. plan		X	X	X			X
G. A. Harvey Off. Frnt.		X	X	X	X	X			X
Howden Steel Equip.				X	X	X			X
Intercraft Designs	X	X	X	X	X	X	X		X
Jetleys (G.B.) Ltd.	X		X	X	X	X	X	X	X
Kalamazoo Ltd.									X
Leabank Office Equip.					X	X			
Libraco Ltd.	Library, museum and lecture room furniture and shelving								
Magowan & Co. Ltd.						X		X	
D. Matthews & Son Ltd.	X	X		X	X	X		X	

Supplier	Box file	Horizontal flat/top	Vertical non-suspension	Suspen. tabbed	Suspen. flat/top	Suspen. lateral	Suspen. vertical vision	Rotating	Misc.
M.B.C. Company		Vertical plan sus.							
E. J. Mellett Ltd.	X					X			X
Mobinet Co. Ltd.				X	X				X
Moore's Modern Methods			X		X	X	X		X
Stuart Murray (Filing) Ltd.	X	X		X	X	X		X	X
National Loose Leaf Co.	X			X	X	X			X
Remington Rand	X		X	X	X	X		X	X
Roneo Vickers Ltd.	X		X	X	X	X	X	X	X
Rotadex Systems Ltd.								X	
Safto Products Ltd.	Metal tabs, misc. accessories and rotating file containers								
Sankey-Sheldon Ltd.	X		X	X	X	X			X
Shannon Ltd.			X	X	X	X			X

Supplier	Box file	Horizontal flap/top	Vertical non-suspension	Suspen. tabbed	Suspen. flat/top	Suspen. lateral	Suspen. vertical vision	Rotating	Misc.
Snowdex Ltd.	X			X	X	X			X
Tacon Bros. Ltd.	X		X						X
T.B.S. (South Wales) Ltd.		X		X	X	X			X
Trade Loose Leaf Co.			X		X				X
Twinlock Ltd.				X	X	X			X
Welconstruct Co.	X	X		X	X	X			X
Western Trading Co.			X	X	X				X
Peter Williams Ltd.	X		X		X	X			X
Frank Wilson (Filing) Ltd.	X	X	X	X	X	X	X	X	X
Jetleys (G.B.) Ltd.	Specializing in computer output storage								
Snowdex Ltd.	Specializing in computer output storage								

Appendix 2: Types of Shelving and Suppliers

Supplier	Shelving	Binding equip.	Shredders	Card index cabinets	Vertical machine accounting files	Rotary files	Card tray files	Strip index files	Punched card filing	Marginal edge punch cards
Alpa Steel & Plastics		X		X	X					
Geo. Anson & Co.		X		X			X	X	X	X
Art Metal	X	X		X		X	X	X	X	
Baird & Tatlock Ltd.	X			X						
Beanstalk Shelving Ltd.	X	and wire trays								
British East-Light Ltd.		X		X						
F. C. Brown Ltd.				X						
Roy Bulmer Ltd.		X		X			X	X		
Carter-Parratt Ltd.				X			X	X	X	X
C. W. Cave & Co. Ltd.		X		X		X	X	X	X	
Copeland-Chatterson Co.				X	X		X	X		X

Supplier	Shelving	Binding equip.	Shredders	Card index cabinets	Vertical machine accounting files	Rotary files	Card tray files	Strip index files	Punched card filing	Marginal edge punch cards
Henry Elwin Ltd.				X						
Expandex Ltd.						X		X		
Flexiform Ltd.	X			X			X	X	X	
J. Glover & Sons Ltd.	X						X			
G. A. Harvey Office Frnt.				X						
Howden Steel Equip.				X						
Intercraft Designs	X			X					X	
Jetleys (G.B.) Ltd.		X				X				
Kalamazoo Ltd.		X			X	X		X		X
Libraco Ltd.	Library and museum shelving									
Magowan & Co. Ltd.		X	X			X				
D. Matthews & Son Ltd.			X	X			X	X		

Supplier	Shelving	Binding equip.	Shredders	Card index cabinets	Vertical machine accounting files	Rotary files	Card tray files	Strip index files	Punched card filing	Marginal edge punch cards
M.B.C. Office Systems				X		X				
E. J. Mellett Ltd.		X		X						
Mobinet Co. Ltd.					X		X			
Stuart Murray (Filing) Ltd.	X	X		X	X	X	X			
National Loose Leaf Co.		X		X				X		
Remington Rand	X			X		X	X	X	X	
Roneo Vickers Ltd.	X	X		X				X		
Rotadex Ltd.				X		X	X		X	
Sankey-Sheldon Ltd.	X	X	X	X					X	X
Shannon Ltd.		X		X	X		X	X		
Snowdex Ltd.		X		X						
Tacon Bros. Ltd.				X						

Supplier	Shelving	Binding equip.	Shredders	Card index cabinets	Vertical machine accounting files	Rotary files	Card tray files	Strip index files	Punched card filing	Marginal edge punch cards
T.B.S. South Wales				X						
Trade Loose Leaf Co.		X					X	X		
Twinlock Ltd.		X					X	X		
Welconstruct Co. Ltd.	X			X			X	X		
Western Trading Co.				X	X					
Peter Williams (Filing) Ltd.	X	X		X				X		
Frank Wilson (Filing) Ltd.	X	X			X	X		X		

Appendix 3: Alphabetical List of Suppliers

Abbott Bros. (Southall) Ltd.,
Abbess Works,
Southall,
Middlesex.

Alpa Steel & Plastics Ltd.,
240–254 Maybank Road,
London, E.18.

George Anson & Co. Ltd.,
Solway House,
Southwark Street,
London, S.W.1.

Art Metal,
199–203 Buckingham Palace
    Road,
London, S.W.1.

Baird & Tatlock (London)
    Ltd.,
Welwyn Metal Products
    Section,
80–86 Bridge Road East,
Welwyn Garden City,
Hertfordshire.

Beanstalk Shelving Ltd.,
Chichester,
Sussex.

British East-Light Ltd.,
P.O. Box No. 3,
32 Broadway,
Barking,
Essex.

F. C. Brown (Steel Furniture)
    Ltd.,
Queens Road,
Bisley,
Surrey.

Roy Bulmer Ltd.,
13 Essex House,
George Street,
Croydon,
Surrey.

Carter-Parratt (Visirecord)
    Ltd.,
Orchard Road,
Sutton,
Surrey.

C. W. Cave & Co. Ltd.,
Greenhill House,
90–93 Cowcross Street,
London, E.C.1.

The Copeland-Chatterson Co.
    Ltd.,
Gateway House,
1 Watling Street,
London, E.C.4.

Henry Elwin Ltd.,
Plumptree Street,
Nottingham.

Expandex Ltd.,
Hitchin Street,
Biggleswade,
Beds.

Flexiform Ltd.,
69–73 Theobalds Road,
London, W.C.1.

J. Glover & Sons Ltd.,
Leacroft Works,
Queens Road,
Egham,
Surrey.

G. A. Harvey Office Furniture
   Ltd.,
Villiers House,
Strand,
London, W.C.2.

Howden Steel Equipment,
173 Maclellan Street,
Glasgow, S.1.

I.C.C. Machines Ltd.,
Alexandra Road,
Enfield,
Essex.

Intercraft Designs,
Berkeley Square House,
Berkeley Square,
London, W.1.

Jetleys (Great Britain) Ltd.,
172 Buckingham Palace Road,
London, S.W.1.

Kalamazoo Ltd.,
Northfield,
Birmingham 31.

Leabank Office Equipment
   Ltd.,
Woden Road,
Wolverhampton.

Libraco Ltd.,
Lombard Wall,
Woolwich Road,
Charlton,
London, S.E.7.

3M Company,
3M House,
Wigmore Street,
London, W.1.

Magowan & Co. Ltd.,
13 Dudley Road,
Wolverhampton,
Staffs.

D. Matthews & Son Ltd.,
P.O. Box 81,
61–63 Dale Street,
Liverpool L69 2DN.

MBC (Office Systems) Ltd.,
Elite Works,
Station Road,
Lawford, Manningtree,
Essex.

E. J. Mellett Ltd.,
Albert Road North,
Reigate,
Surrey.

Metal Details Ltd.,
45–47 South Street,
Bishop's Stortford,
Hertfordshire.

The Mobinet Co. Ltd.,
19 Heneage Street,
Brick Lane,
London, E.1.

Moore's Modern Methods
    Ltd.,
37 Fleet Lane,
Old Bailey,
London, E.C.4.

Stuart Murray (Filing) Ltd.,
Ferry Lane,
Brentford,
Middlesex.

National Loose Leaf Co. Ltd.,
National Works,
Purley Way,
Croydon,
Surrey.

Remington Rand Division,
Sperry Rand Ltd.,
65 Holborn Viaduct,
London, E.C.1.

Roneo Vickers Ltd.,
Roneo House,
Lansdowne Road,
Croydon CR9 2HA.

Rotadex Systems Ltd.,
5 Fortnum Close,
Kitts Green,
Birmingham 33.

Safto Products Ltd.,
Gunnels Wood Road,
Stevenage,
Herts.

Sankey-Sheldon Ltd.,
GKN House,
22 Kingsway,
London, W.C.2.

The Shannon Ltd.,
Shannon Corner,
New Malden,
Surrey.

Snowdex Ltd.,
47–49 Tudor Road,
Hackney,
London, E.9.

Tacon Bros. Ltd.,
8–10 Burwell Road,
London, E.10.

T.B.S. (South Wales) Ltd.,
Triumph Works,
The Willows,
Merthyr Tydfil,
Glamorganshire.

Trade Loose Leaf Co. Ltd.,
Guidex Works,
Bradford Street,
Birmingham 12.

Twinlock Ltd.,
Twinlock Works,
Croydon Road,
Beckenham,
Kent.

The Welconstruct Co. Ltd.,
Camden House,
Parade,
Birmingham 1.

The Western Trading Co.
(London) Ltd.,
4–8 North Road,
Southall,
Middlesex.

Peter Williams (Filing
Systems) Ltd.,
Briset House,
Briset Street,
London, E.C.1.

Frank Wilson (Filing) Ltd.,
Railex House,
13 City Road,
London, E.C.1.

Index